CW01500831

The Amethyst Programme:

Validating your body, mind and spirit after trauma and abuse

Dr Jessica Taylor

By the same author

Taylor, J. (2024) The Watcher of Your Own Flame: Understanding and nurturing yourself after trauma

Taylor, J. (2024) Underclass: A Memoir, Hachette, Little, Brown Publications, London

Taylor, J. & Shrive, J. (2023) The Indicative Trauma Impact Manual, VictimFocus Publications, London

Taylor, J. (2022) Sexy but Psycho: How patriarchy uses women's trauma against them, Hachette, Little, Brown Publications, London

Taylor, J. (2020) Why Women are Blamed for Everything: Exposing the culture of victim blaming, Hachette, Little, Brown Publications, London

Taylor, J. (2020) The Reflective Journal For Parents and Carers: Supporting your child after sexual abuse, VictimFocus

Taylor, J. & Shrive, J. (2020) The Primary School & Home School Guide: Ethical sex and relationships education for young children, VictimFocus

Taylor, J. (2020) Woman in Progress: The Reflective Journal for Women and Girls Subjected to Abuse and Trauma, VictimFocus

Taylor, J. (2020) The Reflective Journal for Researchers and Academics, VictimFocus

Taylor, J. (2019) The Reflective Journal for Practitioners Working in Trauma and Abuse, VictimFocus

The Amethyst Programme:

Validating your body, mind and spirit after trauma and abuse

Dr Jessica Taylor

VictimFocus

Publications

The Amethyst Programme was created by Dr Jessica Taylor to provide a trauma-informed, anti-pathology, anti-blaming, holistic approach to validating ourselves after trauma – even when no one else will.

Therapy works for some people, but not for others. Therapy is accessible and affordable for some people, and not for others. We are taught that the only route out of our trauma is traditional therapies – meaning we are always at the mercy of those services, professionals, policies and theories.

For some of us, deep reflection, finding answers to our questions, learning more about our bodies and minds, and exploring ourselves is key to moving on from trauma.

This programme seeks to give the power and the knowledge back to women and girls through reflection, thought, knowledge, and ideas.

Content

Introduction

Welcome to The Amethyst Programme!

Thank you for embarking on this transformative journey with us. Your decision to explore this resource is a profound act of courage and self-care, and we are honoured to walk alongside you on your path toward healing and empowerment.

This book is designed to complement our comprehensive course offered at VictimFocus. However, we understand that not everyone can, or wishes to, engage in the course. For that reason, this resource stands independently, allowing you to navigate its contents at your own pace and in your own way.

Why The Amethyst Programme?

The Amethyst Programme was created as an alternative to conventional pathways to healing - a space for women and girls who seek a trauma-informed, feminist, and holistic approach. We recognise that healing is deeply personal and that traditional options like therapy or medication, while life-changing for some, may not suit everyone. For others, these methods may even feel harmful, inaccessible, or incongruent with their individual needs and values.

At the heart of The Amethyst Programme is a simple yet powerful principle: knowledge is power. For far too long, women and girls have been told that their healing depends on external authorities - professionals, systems, or institutions. While these supports can be invaluable, we believe true empowerment comes when women are equipped with the knowledge, tools, and skills to lead their own healing journeys.

This programme is not about prescribing a one-size-fits-all solution. Instead, it offers you the freedom to explore, process, and grow in ways that feel authentic to you. Whether you choose to engage with traditional methods, use this programme as a stand-alone resource, or combine approaches, the choice is entirely yours.

Why 'amethyst'?

The amethyst crystal holds deep spiritual and symbolic significance. Known for its calming and protective properties, amethyst has long been associated with clarity, resilience, and healing. Its structure symbolises strength and transformation, reflecting the core of this programme. Just as the amethyst crystal supports those who work with it, this programme seeks to guide you toward healing, self-discovery, and renewal.

Why thirteen steps?

The number 13 carries profound spiritual significance, particularly for women. In many ancient traditions, 13 is considered a divine number, closely tied to the cycles of the moon and the rhythms of nature. A year contains 13 perfect lunar cycles, mirroring the natural flow of feminine energy.

By structuring The Amethyst Programme around 13 steps, we honour these connections, grounding your healing journey in wisdom, intuition, and balance.

The Amethyst Programme is more than a resource, it's an invitation to reclaim your power, reconnect with your inner self, and heal in a way that feels right for you. Whether this is your first step or part of a longer journey, know that you are not alone. This space is yours to explore, create, and transform.

Let's begin.

We understand that sharing your experiences can feel vulnerable, intimidating, or even unsafe. The fear of being judged, misunderstood, or dismissed often prevents women and girls from seeking the help they need. The Amethyst Programme was specifically designed to honour your privacy, providing a safe and confidential space where you can process your emotions and experiences on your terms.

We work from an anti-pathology, trauma-informed approach – which means there is no labelling, no blaming, no shaming and no judging in this programme.

If at any point you feel too triggered, distressed, upset or you are in danger from someone around you, including the need of urgent mental health support, please contact the relevant authorities in your area, or talk to someone you can trust.

The Amethyst Programme was designed by me (Dr Jessica Taylor). I am a British feminist and trauma-informed, anti-pathology psychologist who works to challenge pathologisation and victim blaming of women and girls who have been through various traumatic experiences including abuse and violence. I am also an author, a lecturer, speaker and consultant on trauma, violence and abuse.

Alongside me in this programme, is my wife and co-author Jaimi Shrive. Together we run our international company, VictimFocus (you can look up all our free resources on victimfocus.com), and we co-authored the first anti-pathology, trauma-informed A-Z of trauma responses and coping mechanisms together back in 2023. The Indicative Trauma Impact Manual is available worldwide.

Jaimi has contributed to this programme, and written some of the steps you will take as you work through, so I wish to thank her for her valuable words and ideas.

Take your time with this programme, and let me know how you get on!

All my love to you,

Dr Jessica Taylor

Step 1: Exploring my trauma types

The Amethyst Programme is written to include many different forms of trauma – and with that in mind, in Step 1, I would like to invite you to consider the many different distressing and traumatic experiences you have had in your life. It is, after all, very unlikely that you have only had one distressing thing happen to you.

Take your time with this step, as you may find that you have lived through much more than you have ever stopped to consider.

Different types of trauma will have different impacts on each of us.

It sounds so obvious, doesn't it? We are all individuals, and all of our experiences were individual, too. There is no 'standard', and there is no one-size-fits-all.

Two people could experience the exact same traumatic event, and respond totally differently. One of those people might not even find it particularly distressing, whilst the other person might feel that it has totally derailed their life.

Not only are our responses unique to each of us, but the nature of the traumatic incident is likely to give rise to totally different trauma responses and coping mechanisms.

It is arguably a very different form of trauma to be trapped in a house fire, to being told that your child has a brain tumour, for example. Being abused by your parents for your whole childhood is going to have a different impact than being in a car crash.

There are many factors that make up each of the thousands of possible traumas we can all live through.

Some examples of traumas we could live through are below, but are in no way an exhaustive list:

Abortion	Divorce	Loss
Accidents/injuries	Domestic abuse	Medical procedures
Adoption	Drowning	Menopause
Assaults	Emotional abuse	Military service
Bereavement	Eviction	Neglect
Being arrested	Failure	Nursing
Being bullied	Favouritism	Orphaned
Burglary	FGM	Pathologisation
Child abuse	Forced marriage	Periods
Child sexual abuse	Forced therapy	Police brutality
Civil unrest	Forced medication	Poverty
Classism	Foster care	Pregnancy
Coercive control	Fraud	Puberty
Conversion therapy	Grief	Racism
Cults	Harassment	Rape
Cyberstalking	Heart attack	Refugee
Death of a pet	Homelessness	Repatriation
Death of family	Homophobia	Ritual abuse
Debt	'Honour' abuse	Robbery
Deportation	House fire	Self-harm
Diagnostic tests	Illnesses	Sexual violence
Discrimination	Jury duty	Vicarious trauma

Rather than seeing trauma as rare, or in some way shocking, I personally work from the position that traumatic life experiences are very common, and that every single one of us will experience something traumatic in our lives. For many of us, we will experience several traumas – for some of us, it will be hundreds of traumas.

When it comes to trauma factors that shape how we will respond and cope include when it happened, how it happened, who was involved, whether any types of violence and abuse were used, whether we were psychologically manipulated, whether we were threatened, how long it happened for, whether we remember it, whether we understood it at the time, whether we normalised it, how it ended, whether there was intervention or action taken, whether we were believed or blamed, whether we ever received support, and whether we were protected.

Trauma can impact your education, social skills, cognitive skills, friendship groups, attainment, opportunities, self-confidence, physical health, reproductive health or psychological well-being.

Did the trauma occur when you were a baby, a toddler, a small child, a pre-teen, or a teenager? Did it transcend multiple developmental periods, and impact the formation of your sense of self, your sense of safety, your belief systems, your connection to your religion or culture, your sexuality or your identity?

Or did it happen to you in adulthood? Did it disrupt your life and your goals? Did you feel you got knocked off your path, or were you already feeling pretty lost when you went through the trauma?

As you can see just from this small section (which is in no way exhaustive), the answers to these possible factors will be different for everyone.

If our trauma arose from accidents or injuries, there are many other factors to consider, each of them causing a different kind of trauma response and coping mechanism.

Factors could include what kind of accident we experienced, whether we were alone at the time, whether we can remember it happening, how much pain we were in, how fast emergency help got to us, whether we thought we were going to die, whether we lost consciousness, whether we suffered significant blood loss, whether we became trapped, whether we had to escape from somewhere, whether others were also involved in the accident, whether we saw other people injured or dying, when it happened, why it happened, how it happened, and whether we have scars or lifelong injuries that we have had to adjust to.

Accidents and injuries can be life-altering, not just in the physical sense of the impact on the human body, but also with regards to our psychological responses to the incident. It is common and natural for us to carry trauma from accidents and injuries for many years of our lives, and for us to make (through choice, or as an implication of the injuries) significant changes to our behaviours, hobbies, sports, and lifestyles.

On top of everything else, some of us will experience illnesses, diseases and health issues that will deeply distress and traumatise us. Again, these journeys are all unique for each of us, and if you relate to this section, you are likely to have a unique and personal answer to the next paragraph.

Some factors that may shape our trauma responses to illnesses and health issues include how severe the symptoms are, what kind of illness we have, the diagnostic process, our relationship with health care professionals, how we are treated by health services, whether we were taken seriously about our health concerns, how we were diagnosed, when we were diagnosed, how our loved ones responded, how we felt about our loved ones seeing us suffer, whether our income and employment was affected, whether we had financial dependents, how much pain we are/were in, whether there was a chance we could have died, whether we became permanently disabled, whether our illness is curable, whether our illness required surgery, whether our illness is terminal, whether the treatment was harmful or difficult to undertake, whether we had support and resources during our illness, whether we understood what was happening to us, how long the illness lasted, how long it took to receive the correct treatment, whether we were subjected to medical malpractice or discrimination when we sought help, whether we were frightened of medical services, and whether our illness caused us to question our belief systems.

Again, this list is not exhaustive, but serves to give a small insight into the wide variation of factors that change our experiences of our trauma, and ultimately change how we respond, and how we try to cope.

For some of us, our traumas come from being subjected to an assault or crime – and can be one of the most traumatic incidents of our lives.

Crime, is of course, very broad.

When I write about crime in this section, I mean anything from being robbed or burgled through to being a victim of knife crime. I include all forms of single incident assaults, fraud, homicide, robbery, burglary, sexual offences, hate crimes, criminal damage, offences with weapons, terrorist incidents, and being spiked - but generally, I speak in this section of incidents that happened once, and there was a clear beginning and ending.

Any one of those crime types will produce specific trauma responses, caused by the very nature of the crime. Having our drink spiked and sexually assaulted by a stranger is likely to cause different trauma responses to waking up in the middle of the night to a burglar in our house.

Having worked with victims of crime for fourteen years, I know the vast and varied reactions people have to being targeted, but some factors that I have seen shape the trauma of the person are below.

We are likely to see different trauma responses and coping mechanisms develop depending on whether the crime was violent or not, whether weapons were used, whether there was threat to life, whether there was injuries to self and/or others, whether anyone was killed in front of us, whether we tried to fight back or intervene, whether we remember what happened, who the perpetrator was, how fast it happened, when it happened, where it happened, whether anyone helped us, whether we reported to police, whether we witnessed crime against someone else, how old we were at the time, whether we had to go to court, whether the perpetrators were arrested or convicted, whether the perpetrator was known to us, whether we were in a public place, whether the crime involved breaking into our personal space or home, whether we were hospitalised, whether the crime was linked to our ethnicity or religion, whether we were blamed or disbelieved, how fast emergency services attended the scene, how we were treated by police or other professional services, whether we sought support, whether the incident impacted our personal lives, our physical health, our mental health, our social lives, our careers and employment, our income and resources, our belief systems, and many other factors.

Huge, huh?

And what if the crime or assault are repetitive and ongoing?

This chronic and ongoing trauma is common in all forms of domestic, sexual and child abuse, bullying in childhood and adulthood, stalking, harassment, being held hostage, tortured, kidnapped, and prolonged, ongoing, repeated incidents.

Factors to consider here are related to the length of time - and ultimately - the nature of the crimes which cause the trauma to become cumulative, multilayered and multifaceted. Whilst just one single incident of crime can be life-changing, it is important to understand that when you have been abused, stalked, or bullied for months or years, you have been subjected to many traumas, one after the other, without any space or safety to process the last. I do feel that we sometimes lump hundreds of traumas into one label such as 'child abused', sexual abuse' or 'domestic abuse'. Whilst this isn't the intention, it means that I have worked with hundreds, maybe thousands, of people who haven't had their numerous traumas validated, because everything that had ever happened had been lumped into one big 'trauma'.

However, whilst there is the potential for hundreds or even thousands of unique traumas, we tend to lump it all in under 'domestic abuse' - which never truly captures the variety of traumatic incidents and environments we have lived in for months, years or even decades of our lives.

With that said, factors I would consider here would be how long the abuse lasted, when it happened, when it started and ended, how it started and ended, whether it changed in severity over time, what different kinds of assaults, abuses, stalking and bullying were included over the time period, who the perpetrator was, what kind of grooming and control tactics they used, whether we were isolated from family and friends, whether children were involved at any level, whether there was repeated or ongoing threat to our life, whether there was use of suicide threats from the perpetrator, whether we understood what was happening to us, whether we blamed ourselves or felt we were causing their behaviour towards us, whether we ever tried to escape and what happened when we did, whether we reported to police or authorities, how we were treated when we told people, whether we loved or were in love with our perpetrator, whether the abuse or bullying was covered up or hidden by someone, whether we were outcast from our families, whether we became pregnant, gave birth or had miscarriages during or caused by the abuse, whether anyone knew what was happening to us, whether anyone tried to intervene or protect us, whether the perpetrator was protected in some way, whether we had to move house, run away, try to escape or go into a refuge for safety, and whether we had to try to protect others from the same perpetrator (such as our children, siblings or other loved ones).

No wonder we are all battling such complicated and unique experiences in our lives - and no wonder the one-size-fits-all medical mental health model doesn't work!

And we haven't even gotten into grief, poverty, oppression and discrimination - which would easily have 20-50 factors each.

No matter the traumatic incident, I hope I have demonstrated here how unique our experiences of trauma truly are. Whether you experienced a still birth, nursed your dying relative, volunteered in a war zone, were subjected to female genital mutilation, spent years working in emergency services, went bankrupt, your house was destroyed in a flood, you buried your own child, were sexually harassed by your driving instructor, watched your mother be beaten up every day by your father, or lived in care homes and foster homes until you ran away - every experience we have is unique to us, and so is our trauma.

Learning more about the factors that shaped our experiences can give us clues and insight into our own responses and coping mechanisms.

For me, I must say that this strategy was something I came to naturally, and applied to myself consistently over many years. I wanted to share this with you here in case it was useful - but mostly because I feel strongly that in order for us all to support ourselves through traumatic times in our lives, we must become an expert on our own life experiences.

We must be able to look back at those moments in our lives with love and honour for ourselves, and with a willingness to understand what was happening to us, around us, and for us, so we can start to unpick our relationship with our body, mind and spirit.

Use this space to list the different types of trauma you have experienced in your life so far.

Out of all of the types of trauma you have experienced, which do you think impacted you the most and why?

Do you think that different types of trauma cause different responses in people when you disclose to them? Why/why not?

Are there any types of trauma you have experienced that you feel you dealt with better than others? Why do you think this might be?

What do you think the most 'taboo' form of trauma is? Why do you think this?

If you have experienced multiple different types of trauma in your life, which one changed the way you see the world the most?

Some people go through life having been subjected to many traumas, but not really identifying or acknowledging them for what they were. Do you think this applies to you?

How do you feel your traumas have overlapped over time?

Do you feel there is any pattern or repetition in the traumas you have experienced in your life?

On reflection, do you feel you held any preconceived ideas about certain traumas before you personally experienced them?

How do you think traumas arising from illness and accidents differ from traumas arising from violence and abuse?

Some people say that the way they were treated when they disclosed trauma was worse than the trauma itself. Does this resonate with you at all?

Which of your traumas has been the hardest to process or
move on from? Why do you think this is?

Way to go! You completed the first step, 'Exploring my trauma types'. Awesome work.

Write one thing you learned about yourself from this step.

Write one thing that challenged you to think differently in this step.

Remind yourself how proud you are that you are choosing to work through this programme. Go on, give yourself some love!

Step 2: Why did this happen to me?

The second step of *The Amethyst Programme* is to explore our feelings about *why* the trauma happened. Why did this happen to me? Why did this person harm me? Why was I so badly let down? Why was a put at such risk? Why does it keep happening? Why do I keep getting sick? Why do I feel so isolated?

We have many questions about our traumas, no matter how they happened.

Those questions can make us feel like we are 'losing our mind' or 'going crazy' – but they are totally normal. It makes sense that we would want answers to why we were harmed, especially when there is a societal narrative that bad things happen to us because we must deserve it in some way.

It is common for us to want closure, to want explanations, and to want apologies, to want consequences, to want reparations, or even, dare I say, revenge.

As part of this questioning process, many of us will eventually come to a point where we start asking why we were subjected to such trauma.

This step encourages you to think about this, in your own time, and in your own words. For some of you, this section may not need much thought, but for others, this section may be one of the most complex to think about. Some of you will have been through traumas where no one person or system was responsible – but for many of you, your trauma was caused by a person or a system of people. So, let's start there.

Why do humans do so much damage to each other?

One of the things that used to perplex me the most, is how humans have become so toxic, violent and harmful to each other for no evolutionary reason. Animals are violent to each other, but usually, there is a reason for their behaviour. Maybe they are protecting their young, or marking their territory. Maybe they are hunting for food to survive. Humans, however, seem to torture each other for fun.

Key theories about why humans cause harm to each other often centre around social, psychological, and evolutionary explanations. Social learning theory suggests that individuals learn violent behaviour through observation and imitation, especially when these actions are normalised (and even sensationalised) within their environment.

Psychological theories, like the frustration-aggression hypothesis, argue that frustration in life can lead to aggression when individuals perceive a threat to their goals.

Evolutionary psychology proposes that aggressive behaviours may have developed as survival mechanisms, allowing humans to compete for resources or protect themselves (which is similar to what I said about animals, I guess).

Cognitive dissonance theory suggests that when people's actions conflict with their beliefs, they might rationalise their harmful behaviours to resolve the tension.

Finally, systems of power and control, such as patriarchy and social hierarchies, can perpetuate harm by reinforcing dominance and oppression. It is probably unlikely that any one theory is correct (as usual!) but together, these theories highlight the complex interplay between environment, psychology, and societal structures in explaining human violence.

Despite us having all these theories, I have so many unanswered questions. For example, if we agree with social learning theory in 2024, that makes total sense in a world drenched in violent movies, video games and Netflix investing millions of dollars into 'true crime' and 'serial killer' dramas and docuseries to pump out across the world – but crucially, there is a problem with this theory.

If humans all learn violence from each other, did this mean we were always abusive and violent to each other? Since our evolution from animals?

Does this mean we naturally evolved to become increasingly abusive, toxic and harmful as time went on? Were we always this way? Have we ever had a period of our development where we supported and protected each other?

If not, why not?

One possibility arises from using evolutionary theory. If evolutionary theory suggests that we used violence and harm just as animals do (for protection, for territory, for food and resources), then maybe this is correct, and then three things occurred:

1. Humans collectively and individually recognised that violence and harm was powerful, successful, and effective – and so they emulated it and repeated it in their own ways

2. Humans developed neurologically and psychologically, and realised that they could selectively use violence and harm to get something they wanted, not only the things they needed

3. Humans recognised (at some deeper level) that they enjoyed the feeling of harming others, of having power and control over others, and those positive feelings led to positive reinforcement of the behaviour which then continued throughout generations

In addition to these possibilities, it is likely that we learned through experience and storytelling, that violence was celebrated, power became synonymous with violence, and peace was perceived as a form of weakness.

We understood that our dictators and leaders ruled with fear and violence, and everyone did what they said. They lived with riches stolen from other nations. They slept in palaces built by slaves they tortured and murdered. They raped women to get an heir to their thrones, and killed them if they didn't get pregnant. Their vast empires (including the British Empire) were achieved through years of violence, murder, torture, slavery, rape and abuse.

For me, this is where we differ significantly from animals.

Animals may show violence when required, but they have never waged war on each other. They generally don't abuse or murder their own young. They don't destroy their own habitats. They do not enslave one another.

And I certainly cannot think of an example in nature where a male animal kills a female animal because she cannot get pregnant fast enough. Generally speaking, in mammals such as lions or horses, they simply ignore the females that cannot give them what they want.

Its thoughts like these about our violence, that leave me wondering why we think we are so much more 'civilised' and 'evolved' than animals.

Why do people abuse and bully us?

Unfortunately, whilst there is plenty of war, murder, torture and slavery in our world, the most common form of day-to-day violence between us, has to be abuse and bullying.

The reasons behind why humans abuse and bully others are explained through several similar key theories – again encompassing psychological, social, and evolutionary perspectives.

Social learning theory would suggest that individuals learn abusive or bullying behaviour by observing others. This is especially true because abusive actions are often rewarded or go unpunished,

Power and control theory (which is dominant in most feminist theories of abuse) posits that abuse is a means for perpetrators to maintain dominance over their victims, often using tactics like intimidation and manipulation. Of course, in feminist theory, this approach is applied to patriarchal norms, which means the theories focus on the way men (as the dominant sex) abuse women and girls (as an oppressed class). However, power and control exists even in relationships that are not heteronormative.

Social dominance theory views abuse and bullying as a strategy for securing social status or maintaining hierarchies, and evolutionary psychology proposes that abusive and bullying behaviours may have evolved as a means to gain social status or reduce competition, though such behaviours often exceed what would be adaptive in modern contexts.

There are, however, abuse-specific theories of why people harm us – including sex offender theories.

But what about the other forms of harm? The ones with no particular perpetrator?

What about when our loved one dies of a stroke? Or when we have a car accident? Or when we fall down the stairs? What about when we have a miscarriage? Or when we are told we have a terminal illness?

Harm, suffering, and pain are unfortunately all too common across the world, and it's deeply frustrating and heartbreaking to see how often humans fail to support and protect each other. This isn't because we're inherently bad or incapable of compassion - far from it.

Humans have immense capacity for kindness, empathy, and connection. But there are historical, religious, cultural, and systemic factors that have created a world where harm and suffering are perpetuated, and where collective care has not evolved as our primary way of being.

I guess this is one of life's hard truths. We could be so much better, we could be so much more by now. We could care so much more – and we could be supporting each other through the hardest days of our lives.

The Root Causes of Harm and Suffering

Power and control

Much of the harm in the world stems from the human desire for power and control. Throughout history, societies have been built on hierarchies - patriarchy, colonialism, classism, racism, casteism, colourism, sexism, and other systems of oppression - all designed to concentrate power in the hands of a few while marginalising many. These systems thrive on division, exploitation, and the suffering of those at the bottom of the hierarchy. When power is prioritised over care, harm becomes a byproduct of maintaining control – or it becomes the main, and most successful strategy for maintaining control and power.

I think about this a lot. Everything from fairytales to invasions and warfare prioritise using violence and mass murder to gain control and then maintain an environment of paralysing fear to cause compliance. Most Disney films contain murder, for example. We are all groomed into thinking that fighting, killing, stabbing, beating, shooting and seriously injuring people is the way to 'win' and become respected and revered.

It surprises me how little we criticise this – especially considering we plonk our toddlers in front of these seemingly sweet and endearing tales, only to be taught that harm and violence is an exciting route to overcoming problems and taking control. Scary.

Scarcity and survival

This theory has always interested me, but I guess I am a little sceptical about how it applies to the modern day (especially in rich and developed nations). Early humans lived in conditions of scarcity, where survival often depended on competition for resources like food, shelter, and safety. While we've progressed technologically, the theory suggests that this scarcity mindset has lingered, creating systems that reward greed and hoarding over sharing and equity. Economic inequality, for example, is a modern manifestation of this mindset, where the suffering of many is seen as an acceptable cost for the wealth of a few.

One of the issues I have found with this theory is that people tend to blame it on some sort of genetic or epigenetic predisposition, like a hangover from a less developed time in our history. However, I look around me and see that greed and hoarding resources is not genetic at all – we don't tend to see this behaviour in very small children, for example. We also have cultures and tribes around the world that do not encourage this behaviour and therefore, it does not embed.

Instead, I look around and see capitalism gone wild. We are groomed from an early age to step on anyone and anything to get what we want. Take as much as we can. If it's free, take five. If no one is looking, steal one. Take the piss. Take what you can get. Hoard things. Hoard items. Hoard money. Save it all up. Buy a house. Sell it. Buy a bigger house. Sell that. Buy a bigger house. Buy hundreds of items of clothing you'll wear maybe twice. Throw them away when they go out of fashion, and 'treat yourself' to a shopping spree to buy more. Earn money, but always want more money. Work your way up the ladder to become more and more wealthy, but more and more miserable. Even education has been twisted to be about you earning more money – not about increasing your knowledge and wisdom.

Are we really harming each other due to scarcity? What scarcity?

Fear and othering

Fear has always been a powerful driver of human behaviour. Fear of the unknown, fear of difference, and fear of vulnerability have led to a long history of 'othering' - seeing certain groups or individuals as less deserving of empathy or protection. This tendency has been manipulated throughout history to justify harm, whether through war, violence, rape, oppression, slavery, discrimination, or neglect. When we see others as "less than," it becomes easier to turn a blind eye to their suffering.

We dehumanise those we seek to harm and control. We find reasons why we are above them, better than them, more evolved than them. We strip them of their emotions and their minds. In psychology, we call this 'dementalisation', which is used to oppress people by essentially denying their mental lives.

An example of this is when we oppress and sexualise women and girls in porn. We no longer see them as valid human beings with hopes, dreams, fears, ideas, concerns, thoughts and a rich mental internal life – we see them as tits and ass. Something to fuck. Something to watch. An object of desire, of pleasure, of servitude to the watcher, and to whoever is using her body at the time.

For those of you who haven't read my feminist work and have just read that in shock, you might want to go back to my first books '*Why Women are Blamed for Everything*' and '*Sexy But Psycho*' to delve into those topics much more.

However, dementalisation can be done to anyone. As soon as we begin to deny and ignore the mental life of anyone, we are able to dehumanise and depersonalise them, and their suffering doesn't matter, because their suffering doesn't exist, because we don't even think they are capable of suffering – because we don't give a fuck.

For those of you who have been oppressed, trafficked or abused and harmed systematically by someone or a group of people (or an institution), this may feel very familiar.

Trauma begets trauma

This is a complicated one. Does it really? I don't believe that trauma causes us to harm others, because I believe that every single act of harm is an active choice that has been made. Trauma doesn't cause us to abuse or harm others – our choices do.

We do. We have free will.

However, many people would understand that at some level, trauma has a way of perpetuating itself. People who have been harmed, neglected, or dehumanised often struggle to break free from the cycles of pain they've experienced, and some of them do go on to harm others. This doesn't mean they're doomed to repeat harm, or that it is inescapable or predestined, but without reflection, support and healing, trauma can manifest as anger, mistrust, or even cruelty for some people.

I don't believe trauma is genetic, and I don't think generational trauma is biological, but I do think that when we are brought up by those who externalise their own distress and issues on to us, we must then work extremely hard to break that cycle to make sure we do not continue abusive and harmful patterns in our own lives (no matter whether we have children or not).

Systems over empathy

Modern societies are often structured in ways that prioritise systems over people. Governments, corporations, media, banks and institutions are designed to maintain order and profit rather than prioritise care and empathy. This means that harm and suffering are often dismissed as 'collateral damage' in service of larger goals. When systems are dehumanising, individuals within them can become desensitised, seeing harm as inevitable or outside their control, and I see this a lot in employees of large organisations and especially in institutions such as the military or police forces. They are so used to being harmed, and desensitised to everyone around them being harmed too, that harm just becomes 'part of the job' or 'what we signed up for'.

This is how atrocities happen.

Why haven't humans evolved to care more?

I wonder about this a lot.

Humans often prioritise immediate needs and goals over long-term well-being. And let's be honest, we are encouraged to do this. This focus on the short term has contributed to environmental destruction, economic inequality, and a lack of investment in preventative care. Supporting and protecting each other requires foresight, compassion, and collective action, which can feel at odds with individual survival instincts.

Over time, harm and suffering have been normalised. Phrases like, "That's just how life is", or, "Life isn't fair" reflect a collective resignation to pain as an unavoidable part of existence. It stops us from processing it. From feeling it. This normalisation discourages people from questioning harmful systems or imagining a world built on care and equity. We just don't realise how often we are groomed into thinking this level of suffering is normal.

Why do so few people ever intervene in harm when they see it?

It's a painful truth that so few people intervene when they see someone being harmed, bullied, abused, or targeted. Whether it happens in public, at work, in schools, or within families, bystanders often choose not to get involved.

For the person being harmed, this inaction will feel like another layer of betrayal - proof that they're alone or that their suffering doesn't matter. I speak to so many people who say that their support network never stepping in or offering to help them was more traumatic than the original trauma. The reasons people don't step in are complex and often tied to fear, social conditioning, and systemic issues.

It takes great courage to ignore everything we have been told and taught to feel, and instead, to stick our neck out and defend those who are being harmed.

One of the biggest reasons people don't intervene is fear - fear of retaliation, of becoming a target themselves, or of making the situation worse. In cases of bullying or abuse, stepping in can feel risky, especially if the person causing harm holds power or influence. This fear is particularly strong in hierarchical environments, like workplaces or schools, where speaking up could jeopardise someone's job, reputation, or safety. Ultimately, and as sad as this realisation is, people often weigh up the personal cost of intervening, and decide that it is too high.

In public situations, fear of physical harm or social backlash often keeps people from acting. Many think, 'What if they turn on me? What if I get it wrong?' These fears, while understandable, often paralyse people into inaction, leaving the person being harmed to face the situation alone.

The bystander effect is a theorised psychological phenomenon where the more people witness harm, the less likely any one person is to act. Everyone assumes someone else will step in, leading to a collective paralysis. In a crowd, people often feel less responsible for taking action because they believe it's not solely their job. Humans can become herd animals in situations like this. This diffusion of responsibility creates a dangerous cycle where everyone waits for someone else to intervene—and no one does.

From such a young age, many of us are taught to mind our own business, avoid conflict, and not rock the boat. This social conditioning can make it hard to step in when we see harm happening, especially if it's happening in a group where others are staying silent. People worry about being judged, ostracised, or seen as dramatic if they speak up.

So, why did this happen to you?

The answer is complex. If someone caused harm to you, only they really know why they did what they did. And if someone did do something to you to traumatise and harm you, you are never, ever to blame. Ever.

If your trauma was not caused directly by another person or system, there may not be any clear answer.

Take a breather before moving on. I do hope this section has given you some ideas for your next set of reflective exercises. And you can always come back to this whilst you are considering your answers, too.

In your own trauma, did a person or system cause the harm towards you? If so, write about the way this has impacted you. If not, and your trauma was not caused by a person or system, write about the absence of 'something to blame' in your trauma.

Write three ways you feel trauma has changed the way you perceive the behaviour of those who cause harm.

How has trauma influenced the way you see suffering and
harm done to others?

Do you feel the media deliberately focusses on traumatic and distressing news? Why do they do this? Does it impact you?

Put yourself in the shoes of someone who harmed you or let you down during trauma. Take a few moments to imagine life from their perspective. What do you believe they were thinking or feeling when they harmed you?

Having been through traumatic experiences in your own life,
do you believe humans are generally good, or generally bad?
Has this changed at all?

Do you believe that humans are being influenced not to care about each other? Why/why not?

How would the world change if we addressed the harm and suffering done to so many people? Do you believe this level of global change is possible?

If you were able to influence global leadership, what would you change in order to protect humans from trauma and abuse?

List three ways you feel media encourages us to harm each other.

How do you feel about the investment, support and
understanding towards those who cause harm in the world,
versus the lack of support for their victims?

If you have ever asked, 'why me?' in relation to your own trauma, what answers did you tell yourself, and do you still believe them to be true?

What myths have you been told, or believed to be true, about why your trauma happened to you, or why someone hurt you?

Way to go! You completed the second step, 'Why did this happen to me?'. That was a heavy one!

Write one thing you learned about yourself from this step.

Write one thing that challenged you to think differently in this step.

Remind yourself why you are choosing to work through this programme. Go on, give yourself a little nudge!

Step 3: Understanding my trauma responses

Welcome to the third step of *The Amethyst Programme*. I have written this section to guide you while you explore your trauma responses and coping mechanisms in more detail.

It's no secret, a distressing experience - whether a one-off or an ongoing traumatic environment - can leave you feeling as if you are a totally different person to the one you remember before the trauma. For some of you, as the trauma started so early in life, it may have left you wondering who you would have become if you had never been so distressed at such a young age.

So why should we explore our own trauma responses?

Maybe this sounds like a bad idea, or something that could destabilise us or hurt us. We are often told that we shouldn't, 'dig it all back up' and to 'leave it behind us', for example.

This is especially prevalent in societies where the medical model of mental health rules supreme, and it is insinuated (or in some cases, we are told directly), that digging up our stuff, examining it and learning about it could cause us to totally lose control of our lives. We could go mad. We could harm ourselves or become suicidal. This manufactured fear of doing the deep work on ourselves that we need to do, leads us to avoid it.

Ultimately, we are left with a population of traumatised and stressed children and adults who experience everything from catastrophic thoughts to palpitations - and no one talks about it, no one asks why it is happening, no one dare asks what it all means, whether we can learn from it, whether it means we are crazy, and if you Google it, you end up on websites telling you that you are having a stroke. Or a psychotic episode. Or angina.

Who knows? We've all been there!

The silence around our suffering rolls on, we internalise it, we become anxious, angry, and fearful. We think we have undiagnosed serious health conditions - or we start regarding ourselves as mentally disordered, psychotic, manic, bipolar, borderline, depressed, or anxious. We are led to believe that the only way we could ever get better, is if we spend years in therapy, or take medication for life.

Contrary to this, I wonder what would happen if we do exactly what we are going to do in this step: provide a safe space to explore our trauma responses and our coping mechanisms without fear, without sensationalism, or medicalisation.

Over the years, I have come to realise that many people are frightened of their own trauma responses. They are frightened of the depths of their own mind, body and spirit. They never thought they could have the thoughts they think, feel the emotions they feel, or behave in ways they have been behaving. They experience physical and psychological sensations and phenomena that they cannot explain, and cannot understand. Their body changes, and so does their mind.

If we remain frightened of this natural trauma process, and leave it shrouded in misinformation and myth, we will continue to blame ourselves, pathologise ourselves, and misunderstand ourselves.

Use this step to reflect on your own trauma responses, coping mechanisms - and how you have changed and evolved as your mind, body and spirit have tried their very best to protect you, support you, distract you, fulfil you and heal you.

Trauma responses during the traumatic event

No matter what the traumatic event was, the way we respond in the moment is rarely what we imagined we would do. I think this may be because we are brought up on images of heroic action, fighting back, escaping, risking our lives and standing up for ourselves. Everything from Disney films to our favourite fairytales are filled with characters who risk life and limb to escape avalanches, wars, burning houses, being shot at with a bow and arrow, being bullied by an evil villain. They fight. They run. They jump off a cliff into a waterfall. They throw themselves out of a moving car.

There are very few stories where the main character freezes, doesn't know what to say, can't think, can't move, can't speak, and then can't really remember what happened because they are so distressed.

This topic always reminds me of the way we create this 'perfect trauma victim' stereotype in our societies – and we all feed into it in our own ways. You know what I mean.

The way we chat to our friends and say, *'If I was in that situation, I would have just told them to fuck off!'*

Or, *'Well, if I was driving in those conditions, I wouldn't have taken that corner so fast!'*

Or, *'I would have been straight to the doctor asking for a second opinion, if that was me! I wouldn't have left it that long!'*

So many of us are there, instantly, with our answers to everything. As if we are infallible. As if we can handle anything life throws at us. As if we would be the person who would remain calm, cool, collected.

Any yet, the reality of our trauma responses during a distressing or traumatic incident are anything but the way we imagine with our friends.

We freeze. We go into shock. Our heart races. We feel sick. We throw up. We cry. We scream. We gasp. We faint. We can't catch our breath. We can't get our words out. We can't take information in. We want to do something, but we can't. We feel trapped. We feel doomed. We feel lost. We feel confused. We doubt ourselves.

Maybe we even go into a state of denial. We lie to ourselves. We lie to others. We cover up how we really feel. We tell ourselves that we are overreacting. We question whether it really happened.

It is important to truly honour and support ourselves when thinking about what we did or said in the moment of the trauma — or, if the trauma was prolonged, in the weeks and months of the traumatic experiences. We do and say things we don't understand, or that we don't agree with.

Our responses during the traumatic experience or incident are totally unique, but they all serve an important purpose.

During a traumatic event, we are likely to experience one (or several, or all) of the following trauma responses:

Fight: The fight response is about confronting or resisting danger, often showing up as anger, frustration, or a strong urge to defend yourself. It can sometimes mean that you will fight back, but can mean arguing back, too.

Flight: The flight response drives you to escape or avoid the threat, manifesting as restlessness, anxiety, or a need to keep busy or move away. It can sometimes mean that you try to escape, run away or get away, but it is not always that physical.

Freeze: The freeze response immobilises you, making you feel stuck, numb, or dissociated as a way of trying to 'disappear' from the danger. Similar to the way animals freeze in danger, we may freeze in order to limit damage to ourselves.

Fawn: The fawn response involves appeasing or people-pleasing to avoid conflict or harm, prioritising others' needs over your own to maintain safety. This might manifest as talking your way out of a situation, begging for forgiveness, bargaining, trying to make the person calm down or laugh.

Flop: The flop response is a collapse into helplessness or surrender, where the body and mind shut down in the face of overwhelming threat. In a flop response, you can become semi-conscious, unconscious, or unresponsive. Your body may go floppy like a rag doll, and you might feel like you lose control of your limbs.

Contrary to many others in my discipline, I do not believe that any of these are 'hardwired' into us, and I don't think that people have a go-to response. I don't think the brain 'goes offline' and I don't think some 'reptilian brain' or 'chimp brain' takes over.

I actually think that our brain very quickly, and very carefully, tries to evaluate which of the trauma responses is the safest. Should you shout for help, or stay still? Should you freeze, or try to talk yourself out of this situation?

Many professionals I have met are convinced that the trauma response kicks in from somewhere deep and innate, and that we do the same thing over and over again no matter the circumstances – but I have worked with thousands of adults and children who have been traumatised, and all I have ever heard is variance.

Even children who have been abused by their parents will be able to remember some incidents where they cried for help and begged their parents to stop, and other times where they froze, stayed silent, and waited for it to be over. The same can be said for domestic abuse, bullying and other forms of violence. There may well be times in your life when you stood your ground, (even though you were terrified), and times in your life when you froze, or tried to bargain with the person who was harming you.

If the trauma came from something other than a person or deliberate action – you may remember trauma responses that differ. Maybe a time when you got extremely angry, but another time when you simply froze, and couldn't get any words out.

I guess what I am saying is that our trauma responses are not 'hardwired' into us, and there is a lot to be gained from understanding how our bodies and minds reacted in moment and situations of trauma. They are not random, and our responses had a purpose – even if they are not clear to us!

We also need to recognise that our trauma responses continue well after the incident is over.

The aftermath of a traumatic event can feel just as overwhelming, confusing, and isolating, especially when you start noticing changes in how you think, feel, and behave. But here's the thing: your reactions do make sense. I promise.

They're not 'crazy,' 'weak,' or 'broken.' They are your body and brain doing their best to protect you, and keep you alive.

Let's start with the basics.

When we experience trauma, our nervous system kicks into survival mode. This is where the 'fight, flight, freeze, flop or fawn' responses come in. These are not choices we consciously make per se – they're instinctive reactions designed to help us cope with immediate danger. The trouble is, even after the danger has passed, our nervous system can get stuck in survival mode, leading to responses that might seem puzzling or 'out of proportion' to others, but are entirely normal for someone who's been through trauma.

Now, this is where psychiatry and clinical psychology position these reactions as irrational – whereas I think they are totally rational to remain. Our fear and trauma responses are not likely to just disappear. There is nothing in nature that would suggest this would be a good idea.

For example, if we have just been attacked, or just had a car crash – I don't think it would make sense from any perspective, for that person to sort of brush themselves off a few hours later, and then go back to being totally calm, unbothered, unfazed and unaffected. It makes sense to me, that they would remain frightened, remain shocked, remain worried, remain confused and remain in pain.

We see this in animals, and don't seem to question it at all.

If our beloved dog is attacked at the park, or our cherished cat was almost ran over by a speeding car – we don't expect them to be okay. We don't pathologise them when they become frightened of the park, or cars. We don't suggest they have mental disorders, or need pills to address some invisible disorder they seem to have developed.

These examples I give here are great for one-off trauma events, but many are not one-offs. Lots of traumas are ongoing. Being bullied is a weekly, daily, hourly experience of trauma – and so it makes sense that the trauma responses remain consistent for weeks or months. Child abuse, domestic abuse and sexual abuse are rarely one-off events – and so again, it makes much more sense for the trauma responses to remain for months or years of our lives.

Even after the traumatic event, our core trauma responses are likely to remain.

Once the immediate threat has passed, you might expect to 'bounce back' or 'move on.' But healing from trauma isn't linear, and those survival responses you developed, don't just disappear overnight.

Here are some more common experiences, in case they are useful to you or others around you:

Intrusive Memories

Flashbacks, nightmares, or intrusive thoughts throughout the day can make it feel like you're reliving the trauma. This isn't your brain trying to torture you – it's trying to process what happened and make sense of it, even if it feels anything but logical. It can be triggered by specific things, but sometimes it is repeating itself because it is being repressed or ignored. Generally speaking, I pay attention to things that replay and replay in my mind, as they are my red flag that something about it is still bothering me that I need to process, explore, or understand.

Hypervigilance

You might feel jumpy, easily startled, or constantly on edge. This is your nervous system staying alert, just in case the danger comes back. It's exhausting, but it's your body's way of trying to keep you safe. We can be tricked into believing that our hypervigilance is pathological and disordered, but this is exactly what our mind and body needs to do in order to keep us from being harmed.

When it feels constant, and you cannot stop these feelings or behaviours, one option is to consider when you feel less hypervigilant, or when you don't feel it at all. It might be around a certain person, in a certain room, in a certain part of the country, or in your car.

Everyone has their own places and people who soothe them, and you are likely to have one – no matter how obscure it is.

Once you notice it, the key to figuring out your hypervigilance is to use a technique called 'exception seeking'. If that safe space is your exception, why is it? What is different about it? Why does it calm you down? Why do you feel safe there?

When you have those answers, you can reverse-engineer the answers to understand what your trauma triggers are in other environments or situations. This technique has helped me, and thousands of people I have supported over the years – and I use it to understand trauma triggers. Try it out!

Emotional Numbness

You might feel detached, like you're watching your life from the outside. This is a freeze response lingering in the aftermath, and it's a way your brain protects you from feeling too much all at once.

Emotional numbness can also come about due to you remaining in shock. Try to remind yourself that shock isn't a singular moment – and you may remain in a state of shock for days or weeks. Some people remain in shock for months, although that is a little rarer.

When we are stuck in a state of disbelief and shock, there is little space for other emotions, and when they do come in, they can be fleeting and tiny. We can start questioning why we haven't cried, why we are not angry, or why we don't seem to be able to feel anything. This in itself can traumatise us further, as we sometimes cannot understand why we are behaving and responding in the way we are.

One way to know if this is happening to you is if you have any of the following thoughts or feelings:

- This cannot be real

- There is no way this is happening

- Am I dreaming? Is this a nightmare?

- They would never do such a thing

- Am I just a terrible judge of character?

- Maybe this is all a huge misunderstanding

- Am I making this up?

Of course, for some of you, this was a trauma response that passed eventually. Once the state of shock slowly moves, we tend to be greeted by an avalanche of emotions which ranged from devastation to confusion, and we realise (whether we are ready for it or not) that it is time to feel everything and face reality.

Difficulty Trusting

Trauma can shatter your sense of safety, making it hard to trust others – or even yourself. You might second-guess people's intentions or feel overly cautious in relationships.

Trust is a foundation of our personal and social lives. Nothing in our lives will feel truly safe without it. We have to trust everything from the locks on our doors to our colleagues at work. To some extent, living a relatively normal life (whatever the hell that is!), relies on us trusting others a great deal more than we realise.

No wonder then, it is so common for that to go wrong for us – and it's no wonder that traumatic events will shake our trust in everything we have ever known.

Partially, this is due to the underlying trust that is required for us to function. We trust the brakes on our car. We trust the pilot of the aeroplane. We trust the doctor to make the right decision about our health. We trust the university to mark our work fairly. We trust our parents to look after us. We trust our kids are telling the truth. We trust our partners won't betray us. We trust that guy in the HGV not to be on his phone. We trust the set of ladders we are stood on not to break. We trust the food we eat is safe. We trust the water we drink is clean. We trust the medication we are given isn't going to kill us.

Trauma will shake some level of deep trust for you, whether it is trust in a human, trust in a system, trust in faith, trust in a law, or trust in yourself – and so you can imagine how much it irritates me that traumatised people who struggle to trust are quickly labelled 'paranoid'.

In my experience, most people who have been called 'paranoid', or even call themselves 'paranoid', are intensely scared of something, usually from a complete breakdown of trust in people or systems of care and power.

If you have ever been called 'paranoid', or have thought you yourself are 'paranoid', take a moment here to consider what was truly frightening you, and where it came from.

Biological changes and responses

Trauma doesn't just mess with your mind – it messes with your natural bodily rhythms and processes, too. After a traumatic event, your nervous system can get stuck in survival mode, which means your body acts like the danger is still happening, even when you're safe. This can be triggered by specific memories, but might just feel constant instead. One of the most noticeable changes is in your stress response system. Your body might pump out adrenaline and cortisol (the stress hormones) at the smallest trigger, leaving you feeling constantly on edge or exhausted from the highs and lows that go on for weeks or months.

You might also notice physical symptoms like headaches, muscle tension, or stomach issues. Ever had that feeling of nausea when you're anxious? That's your gut-brain connection kicking in. Trauma can upset this delicate balance, leading to things like indigestion, stomach ulcers, irritable bowel syndrome (IBS) or chronic digestive problems.

Another common response is sleep disturbance. Your body's still trying to 'stand guard,' so you might find it hard to fall asleep, stay asleep, or feel rested even after a full night. This isn't your body betraying you – it's doing what it thinks it needs to do to protect you. I guess the problem is, sleep deprivation can make things very difficult for you, very quickly.

Biological changes caused by trauma-induced sleep deprivation are significant, and kick in fast.

Skipping one night of sleep might not seem like a big deal – most of us have pulled an all-nighter at some point. But even after just one night, your body starts to feel the effects. You'll likely notice brain fog, poor concentration, and slower reaction times. Emotionally, you might feel irritable or overwhelmed, as your brain struggles to regulate your mood without its usual reset. If trauma is already making you hypervigilant, this can feel even worse – like you're constantly running on empty.

After two nights of no sleep, your body begins to struggle. Your immune system takes a hit, making you more vulnerable to illness. You might feel shaky, have headaches, or notice your heart racing more often. Mentally, you could experience trouble forming clear thoughts or even mild hallucinations, like seeing shadows move in the corner of your eye. If trauma-induced hyperarousal is keeping you awake, your nervous system is essentially running a marathon it hasn't trained for – and it's not sustainable.

By day three, the line between being awake and asleep starts to blur. You might find yourself microsleeping – brief moments where your brain shuts down for a few seconds without you even realising it. This can be dangerous, especially if you're driving or doing anything requiring focus. You're likely to feel emotionally detached, almost like you're watching your life from the outside. For someone living through trauma, this can amplify feelings of dissociation, making it even harder to feel grounded.

Four days without sleep is when things get truly dangerous. Your brain becomes unable to process information properly, and you might experience vivid hallucinations or paranoia. This isn't because you're 'losing it' – it's your brain desperately trying to make sense of the chaos. Your body might feel weak, and your motor skills become severely impaired. Going five days or more without sleep is extremely rare and life-threatening. Your body and brain start to shut down essential functions, and you're at risk of serious health complications like heart failure or immune collapse. Studies suggest that the absolute limit for surviving without sleep is about 10-11 days, but by this point, the damage to your body and mind is profound.

Sleep deprivation hits us in trauma even harder than when it is caused by other reasons such as shift working.

When trauma disrupts your sleep, it's a double-edged sword. Sleep is when your brain processes and heals from difficult experiences, but trauma keeps your nervous system stuck in high alert, making that healing almost impossible. It's a vicious cycle: the more sleep-deprived you are, the harder it is for your body to regulate itself, and the more intense your trauma responses become.

On a deeper level, trauma can then leave its mark on the immune system, making you more prone to illnesses. And while this can feel frustrating, understanding it can be the first step in learning how to work with your body to heal.

When you experience trauma, your body floods with stress hormones like cortisol, keeping your nervous system stuck in overdrive. Over time, this chronic stress can dysregulate not only your sleep, but also your immune response, causing it to turn against healthy tissue, which is a hallmark of autoimmune conditions.

For example, someone who's experienced prolonged trauma, like abuse or neglect, might develop conditions like lupus, Crohn's or rheumatoid arthritis. This isn't about "thinking yourself sick" – it's your body's way of reacting to an environment it perceives as constantly threatening. The inflammation caused by stress hormones can trigger autoimmune flares, making symptoms worse.

Behavioural changes and responses

Trauma shows up in your behaviours, sometimes in ways that even you might not fully understand. Avoidance is a big one. You might go out of your way to avoid people, places, or situations that remind you of the event. For instance, someone who was mugged on a dark street might refuse to go out at night, even if they're with friends or in a safe area. If you were in a car accident, you might refuse to get back in a car.

On the flip side, you might find yourself becoming hypervigilant, constantly scanning for danger. This might mean sitting near the door in a café, keeping the lights on at night, or flinching at sudden noises. It's your brain trying to protect you by staying one step ahead of anything threatening.

Trauma can also lead to impulsive or risky behaviours, like excessive drinking, reckless driving, or overspending. These might seem out of character, but they can be attempts to numb the pain or regain a sense of control. Someone struggling with the aftermath of a traumatic breakup might throw themselves into partying, not because they want to party, but because it feels like the only way to escape their thoughts.

And then there's the opposite: withdrawal. You might find yourself isolating, cancelling plans, or losing interest in things you used to love. Trauma can make it feel like connecting with others or finding joy is impossible – even though it's exactly what you need to start healing.

Different ways of understanding your trauma responses

As I hope is becoming clear, there are many different ways of understanding our trauma responses, and so I wanted to finish this chapter by including some here.

I am well aware that my approach to trauma and suffering is unorthodox and rare. I don't believe in mental illnesses, and I don't believe that we can start to feel better after traumas by taking pills or undertaking treatments such as electroconvulsive therapy.

However, lots of people have different perspectives to me, and they will have their own understanding of what happened to them, and what it all meant.

Understanding trauma and our responses to it is deeply personal, and there's no single 'right' way to make sense of it. What works for one person might not resonate with another, and that's okay. The key is recognising that however you understand your trauma, it's about making sense of your experiences in a way that feels meaningful and empowering to you.

The big question isn't just, "Why did this happen?" but also, "What does this mean for me now?"

For some people, trauma responses are seen as purposeful – as the body and mind doing their best to protect you. And this perspective can be profoundly freeing.

Think about it: when you're faced with danger, your brain and body kick into survival mode, using responses like fight, flight, freeze, fawn, flop, or even total dissociation to keep you alive. These are adaptive, not defective. If you froze during a traumatic event, it wasn't because you failed – it was because your body determined that staying still was the safest option. If you dissociate now when something reminds you of the trauma, it's not because you're weak – it's because your brain learned that sometimes checking out is the only way to cope with overwhelming emotions.

From this lens, trauma responses aren't 'illnesses' or 'disorders'. They're deeply human adaptations. They had a purpose – they helped you survive. This doesn't mean they're always helpful now, though. A response that saved you during trauma might cause challenges in your day-to-day life.

For example, hypervigilance, which kept you alert to danger, might now leave you exhausted, on edge, or struggling to trust others. But even when these responses feel like they're harming us, it is always important to remember that they're rooted in a purpose: protection. Understanding this can shift the way we see ourselves, replacing blame with compassion.

Some people find meaning in viewing their trauma and responses as a lesson to learn. I have certainly struggled to understand this one at times in my life, but I am now much more open minded to what this can mean for people.

This doesn't mean the trauma was justified or 'meant to be' – far from it. But it can be a way of reclaiming agency. You might look at how your experiences shaped your boundaries, your relationships, or your understanding of yourself. You might look back and reflect that you did take that corner too quickly on the day you crashed. Perhaps your trauma taught you to be fiercely protective of your safety, or maybe it made you more empathetic to others who've been through similar pain. This isn't about turning trauma into a 'positive' (because Lord knows I hate that toxic positivity bullshit), but about finding ways to move forward with a deeper understanding of who you are and what matters to you.

Others, though, might reject the idea of finding lessons or purpose in trauma altogether – and that's valid too. I totally get that, and respect that. Trauma is painful, unjust, and often senseless. It's okay to feel like there's nothing to 'learn' from what happened – because in lots of cases, there is nothing for you to learn and nothing you could have done differently. Child abuse. Rape. Domestic abuse. Assault. Trafficking. Being spiked. Being bullied. The lessons are there, but they are not for you!

Some might ask whether trauma responses are useless or whether they harm us more than they help us. The truth is, they're neither entirely helpful nor entirely harmful – they're both, depending on the context and how you see them. For example, dissociation might feel disruptive when you're trying to focus at work, but it might have saved you from unbearable emotional pain during the trauma itself. The key isn't to label these responses as 'good' or 'bad' but to recognise their origins and explore whether they're still serving you now. If they're not, that doesn't mean you've failed – it means you're ready to look for new ways to cope.

Another way to understand trauma responses is to see them as messages. Your body and brain are constantly communicating with you, even if it feels like they're working against you. Anxiety might be your nervous system's way of saying, 'I don't feel safe, we need to get out of here, I don't trust this person'.

Emotional numbness might be a signal that your brain is overwhelmed and needs time to process. Self-blame might be a way to make sense of the senseless, even if it's not accurate. When you approach these responses with curiosity instead of judgment, you can begin to understand what they're trying to tell you.

Finally, and of course, the one approach I do not advocate, is psychiatry. The medical model often frames our trauma responses as illnesses – disorders to be fixed or eliminated. But this approach can feel disempowering. Labelling someone as 'disordered' suggests that their responses are abnormal, when in reality, they're entirely predictable reactions to extraordinary stress. Viewing trauma responses as adaptations or survival mechanisms allows us to honour their origins without pathologising ourselves. It reminds us that we're not broken – we're human.

Ultimately, the way you choose to understand your trauma and your responses is entirely up to you. What matters most is that your perspective helps you move forward in a way that feels supportive and compassionate. Maybe you see your responses as purposeful, maybe as lessons, or maybe as challenges to be gently worked through.

Maybe you're still figuring it out – and that's okay too.

The most important thing to remember is that your trauma responses are part of your story, but they don't define you. Whether they help, harm, teach, or frustrate you, they're a reflection of your resilience, and they are all part of your journey.

They're not signs of weakness or illness; they're signs of survival and development.

And as you move forward, you have the power to decide how to work with them, what meaning they hold, and how they'll shape your life from here.

List your own trauma responses here. Think about the way your body and mind responded to the trauma.

Which of your trauma responses bothers you the most? Why does it trouble you?

Which of your trauma responses seems to most understandable to you? Why is this?

Which of your trauma responses or triggers are the hardest to cope with on a day-to-day basis?

The most common response to trauma is to freeze, with over 70% of women freezing in traumatic situations. Can you think of a time when you froze? Why do you think this was your response?

Which of your trauma responses or triggers have disappeared
or lessened with time? How do you think this happened?

Do you have any trauma responses that you carry shame or embarrassment around? How has this impacted you?

Write three of your trauma responses below, and then consider how they worked to protect you during trauma (even if at first, it is unclear).

Some people say that they struggled with their mental health for years before they realised they were actually struggling with trauma. Does this resonate with you at all?

Have you ever mistaken your trauma responses for something else? What did you think they were?

Which of your trauma responses are you frightened of? How does your fear about your trauma response heighten or worsen the response?

Have you had to suppress your natural responses to trauma?
Why did you have to do this, and how did that impact you?

When was the last time you were triggered into a trauma response? Write about what was happening and why your trauma responses kicked in again.

How have your trauma responses evolved and changed over time?

Some people say that learning more about their trauma responses helped them to understand themselves, and stop seeing themselves as having 'mental health issues'. How do you feel about that?

Way to go! You completed the third step, 'Understanding my trauma responses'. How are you feeling?

Write one thing you learned about yourself from this step.

Write one thing that challenged you to think differently in this step.

Use this space to encourage yourself to work through this programme. Tell yourself how well you are doing!

Step 4: Understanding my coping mechanisms

Wow, you're here at Step Four of *The Amethyst Programme*, already.

How are you doing? Are you ready to explore your coping mechanisms and how they developed?

In my opinion, understanding our coping mechanisms is one of the most compassionate things we can do for ourselves. Coping mechanisms aren't random, and they're not flaws or failures. They're strategies our brains and bodies develop to protect us during difficult times.

Whether it's shutting down emotionally, keeping busy to avoid intrusive thoughts, or turning to certain behaviours for comfort, these responses are rooted in survival. When we take the time to understand them, we can move from feeling ashamed or stuck to recognising our resilience and finding healthier ways to cope.

Here are some examples of coping mechanisms:

Acceptance	Change of views	Forgiveness
Activism	Co-dependency	Freezing
Angry outbursts	Compulsions	Fighting
Anxieties	Criticising the self	Hatred
Apologising	Day dreaming	Hearing voices
Ashamed	Desperation	Hoarding
Attachment issues	Disclosing publicly	Hyperindependence
Avoidance	Disinhibition	Hypervigilance
Belief changes	Dissociation	Intrusive thoughts
Betraying others	Derealisation	Obsessions
Binge drinking	Distracting yourself	Overworking
Binge eating	Drinking alcohol	Peace keeping
Causing conflict	Envy	Perfectionism
Change in goals	Fantasies	Self-sabotage

As you can probably appreciate, this is a tiny fraction of possible coping mechanisms, and when Jaimi and I wrote *The Indicative Trauma Impact Manual* in 2023, we included hundreds in there! Even then, I think we only scratched the surface.

Think about it: every coping mechanism you have exists because, at some point, it worked. I feel very strongly about this, and if you have ever heard me speak or lecture, you will have heard me say this more than once.

Just take a moment to reflect on that. Didn't it work for you at some point?

Our coping mechanisms are not irrational, and they are not disordered – they developed because we needed them, and they remained because they were successful!

Maybe you learned to people-please because it kept you safe in a volatile environment. Or perhaps you dissociate when things get overwhelming because it helped you get through a traumatic event when feeling present was unbearable. These aren't weaknesses – they're adaptive responses to experiences that were too much for you to handle at the time. When we frame coping mechanisms in this way, it becomes easier to approach them with kindness instead of judgment.

Understanding your coping strategies also helps you see where they're no longer serving you. What worked to keep you safe during trauma might now be holding you back in everyday life. For example, numbing out might have protected you during a crisis, but if it's stopping you from connecting with others now, it might be time to explore why. This isn't about blaming yourself or trying to 'fix' yourself – it's about gently noticing the patterns you've developed and deciding if they're still what you need.

There's so much power in being able to say, 'I understand why I do this now!' That understanding creates space for curiosity and change. It allows you to explore the deeper needs beneath your behaviours. If you turn to food, alcohol, or overworking to cope, it's not because you're disordered or broken – it's because you're trying to fill a need for comfort, safety, self-worth, or distraction. By recognising the need behind the action, you can start to meet it in ways that feel healthier and more sustainable.

When you understand your coping mechanisms, you also gain more compassion for yourself. Instead of beating yourself up for procrastinating, zoning out, or avoiding conflict, you can step back and ask, 'What's this about? What is my body or mind trying to protect me from right now?' That shift from self-criticism to self-inquiry is where healing begins. It's a chance to stop fighting yourself and start working with yourself.

This also helps in relationships. When you know your patterns, you can communicate them to others, creating more honest and supportive connections. Instead of feeling stuck in the cycle of reacting, you can learn to pause, reflect, and respond in ways that align with who you want to be, not just how you've been shaped by past experiences.

Ultimately, understanding our coping mechanisms is about recognising that we were always doing the best we could with what we had. That understanding is the foundation for growth, healing, and a deeper connection with ourselves.

Coping mechanisms after trauma are not random; they're deeply meaningful survival strategies. They develop because, in the moment of trauma and its aftermath, your brain and body are trying to do their best to protect you and help you survive overwhelming pain, fear, or stress. These mechanisms might seem puzzling or even harmful at times, but they all serve a purpose – they're ways of adapting to something that felt unbearable.

All coping mechanisms share one main purpose: protection. Whether it's physical, emotional, or psychological, trauma teaches your brain to prioritise safety at all costs. Each response reflects an attempt to manage overwhelming feelings, memories, or situations in a way that feels bearable in the moment.

Coping mechanisms don't mean you're weak, damaged, mentally ill, or broken. They mean your body and mind are trying to navigate something too big to process all at once. They're messages – signals that something inside you needs care, safety, or understanding.

In the short term, these coping mechanisms can be lifesaving. They create distance from pain, establish a sense of control, or provide temporary relief. However, over time, some of them might start to feel limiting or harmful.

Understanding your coping mechanisms isn't about judging them or forcing them to change. It's about recognising their origins and asking, 'Does this still serve me?'

If not, you can gently begin to explore other ways to meet the needs they've been addressing, often for months or years of your life. Whether that's through reflection such as this programme, traditional talking therapy, supportive relationships, hobbies, habits, or self-compassion, the goal isn't to 'fix' yourself – it's to create space for healing in ways that feel right for you.

Socially desirable coping mechanisms

The final thought I want to leave you with is something that Jaimi and I have been teaching in our lectures around the world for several years now:

Some coping mechanisms are socially desirable – and some are not.

You may have never heard of this concept before, but we have found it to be extremely helpful in explaining why some coping mechanisms are discouraged and judged, and why others are encouraged and celebrated – despite them being harmful.

Now before I start, I just want to clarify what I mean when I say 'socially desirable'. I am not saying I agree with this judgement, or that I condone it – but I am saying that in our complicated (and rather toxic) societies, there are behaviours that are seen as desirable, and behaviours that are seen as undesirable – and we are often judged and categorised based on them. When we are trying to cope with trauma, the same thing happens to us.

Here is the table we use in our lectures to our students:

Socially desirable coping mechanisms	Socially undesirable coping mechanisms
Moving on quickly/positively	Becoming depressed and low
Working long hours	Becoming angry
Becoming a perfectionist	Self-harming and suicidality
Studying and gaining qualifications and accolades	Challenging people/systems
Self-pressure to succeed	Demanding justice or support
Helping others, being selfless	Talking openly about trauma
Saying the trauma made you a better person	Drinking and taking drugs
Engaging in toxic positivity	Becoming scared and worried
Dedicating yourself to a cause	Not working or studying
Developing hobbies/interests	Losing interest in hobbies

Take a look at the table above. How many of these coping mechanisms do you relate to? Its likely that you will have a mixture of 'socially desirable' and 'socially undesirable' coping mechanisms.

But what does this all mean for us?

Simply put, nothing is neutral. Everything has meaning and values applied to it. Coping mechanisms are socially constructed, just like 'mental disorders'. What we perceive to be 'healthy coping mechanisms' may just be socially desirable, rather than healthy. It is entirely possible that someone may use socially desirable coping mechanisms whilst profoundly struggling, even though everyone around them perceives them as coping brilliantly and healthily.

As an example that I am comfortable sharing with you, after years of trauma in my own life, I became absolutely fixated on work, study, my career, my success, and building wealth.

This came from three main traumas and responses: feeling worthless, feeling overlooked, and feeling trapped in poverty.

I worked more than full time, took on all overtime and extra tasks I could which amounted to around 50-60 hours per week at work. I drove home, I picked the kids up from afterschool clubs and nurseries, got them bathed and ready for bed. Cooked dinner. Got everything ready for the next day. I studied for my degree and then my PhD each evening after the kids were in bed, usually until around midnight (but honestly, sometimes until around 2am). On top of all of this, I wrote articles, blogs, made social media content, AND I used to run a few miles per day in the tiny space I had between dropping the kids off at school and beginning my work day, which started at 09:45. I studied and worked extra on weekends, and out of the eight years I lived like this, I volunteered for five of those years on a mental health project I set up, which grew to an organisation employing 20 people… which I then became the Chair of.

To the outside world, I looked like some kind of superhuman alien wizard thing. Time didn't seem to apply to me. No one could work out how the hell I was doing it.

In the years that passed, I wrote two books per year, several of which became huge bestsellers. I wrote hundreds of resources and training programmes. I appeared on several Netflix documentaries, international news channels, radio shows and famous podcasts. I worked with celebrities and politicians from around the world. I went on book tours across Australia and New Zealand.

People meet me and just stare at me. They realise I am just this average looking 30-something woman, and say, "You are such an inspiration, I want to be just like you! Look at everything you have done!"

And I cringe. I recoil. I never know what to say. Because I know from the outside, my coping mechanisms look fantastic – but on the inside, they have been destroying me for years. My health and my body has taken the brunt of it, but more recently, the impacts have started to overwhelm me.

I guess the reason I wanted to explain this to you in the programme, is because my coping mechanisms are 'socially desirable', and so no one has really noticed that I have spent years trying to fill holes in my life due to my trauma – they have instead believed I am 'healed' and 'strong'.

The reality is much different, and yet, had I not realised what I was doing and put the brakes on back in 2023, I would have probably had a heart attack and died young. I still wonder if that will happen, if I am brutally honest with you.

I did definitely use lots of the socially 'undesirable' coping mechanisms too, but I became better at hiding those when I was younger. I also got more rewards and reinforcement from the 'desirable' mechanisms, so whilst I did drink heavily and take drugs as a teenager, I stopped when I was seventeen, and never did it again. I did definitely engage in some self-harm up to around nineteen years old, but it didn't give me the same fulfilment as achievement, so I stopped that too.

I did become absolutely obsessed with losing weight (hence why I was running miles every morning for years), which resulted in me becoming extremely ill with pneumonia that my body couldn't fight off when I was very thin and not eating in 2015 – but of course, everyone just thought I looked so much better thinner than when I was bigger, that no one actually noticed that I had developed an eating disorder.

The reason I have chosen to share this with you is to encourage you to explore which of your coping mechanisms have been socially desirable – and which have not. I would like you to reflect on which of your coping mechanisms serve others, or even benefit others!

Do you overwork? Do you look after your family? Are you selfless and never put yourself first? Do you always help others, even when you need help yourself? Do you support everyone else at work, even though no one supports you? Is everyone else benefiting from your coping mechanisms? Think about it during this step.

And what about the socially 'undesirable' coping mechanisms?

Aren't they just about you causing some form of inconvenience to a person or a system? Are they actually unhealthy or negative ways of coping, or do they just force people to notice you and help you?

If your coping mechanisms have been to show your emotions, to stop working, to write complaints, seek justice, demand help, to feel suicidal and to seek apologies from those who hurt you, you can see why others would perceive that as problematic!

They would much rather you stayed silent and stopped challenging them. I am sure they would much rather you become a perfectionist, worked fifty hours a week and took up knitting!

The issue here isn't your coping mechanisms, but the way they are treated by others. Friends. Family. Partners. Professionals. Systems.

They prefer us to use coping mechanisms that mean we suffer quietly, with a smile on our face – and this has profound impact on all of us. When we try to disclose and tell the truth of our suffering, many of us are met with horror, judgement and blame. We are regularly told that we need to just 'get over it' and 'move on' – not because that is the right thing to do, but because it means other people don't have to do anything to help us.

Take some time to reflect on all I have said here, and how this plays a role in your own life. I have included some reflective exercises on this topic too, in case you need some space to explore further.

What do you do to cope with the trauma? What are your coping mechanisms?

Think about the section about 'socially desirable coping mechanisms' – do you have any coping mechanisms that probably seem healthy or positive to others, even if they affect you?

Which of your coping mechanisms are related to feelings of helplessness, or hopelessness?

Which of your coping mechanisms are connected to feeling worthless or self-hatred?

Which of your coping mechanisms are related to fear, and a need for control and safety?

Do you have any coping mechanisms that make your life harder? Write about them here.

List three coping mechanisms here. Then write next to them when they developed, and why they developed.

Do you have any coping mechanisms that you are grateful for, or proud of? What are they, and how have they helped you?

Do you have any coping mechanisms that other people perceive as harmful, but you find helpful and effective? What are they?

Do you have any coping mechanisms that are actually about avoidance? Do you do or say anything that means you don't have to address certain traumas?

Which of your coping mechanisms are protecting you from something? What are they protecting you from?

Which of your beliefs and behaviours have you begun to realise are actually coping mechanisms for your trauma?

Do you have any coping mechanisms that appear socially
desirable to the outside world, but are actually harming you?

What do you wish you could explain to people about your coping mechanisms?

What do you feel you still need to learn about your coping mechanisms?

Way to go! You completed the fourth step, 'Understanding my coping mechanisms'. How did it go?

Write one thing you learned about yourself from this step.

Write one thing that challenged you to think differently in this step.

Use this space to encourage yourself to work through this programme. Tell yourself how well you are doing!

Step 5: The impact of trauma on my mind

Welcome to this step of *The Amethyst Programme*!

The impact of trauma on our mind is often profound, but I have noticed that people mistake these impacts for medical issues, illnesses, neurological issues, and even mental disorders.

Trauma isn't just something that happens to us, it embeds into us. It becomes a part of us, whether we like it or not, and it definitely will have some form of impact on our mind, our thinking, decision making, judgement, cognitive abilities, memory, attention spans and focus.

We are very likely to deal with intrusive thoughts, trauma memories, and changes in the way we think. None of these impacts are abnormal or constitute a disorder. Instead, I want to use this fifth step to explore the changes we may experience in our minds during and after trauma – in a way that validates those changes as real and tangible, but does not seek to position them as abnormal or unhealthy.

What I hope to cover here includes memories and flashbacks, fatigue, decision making and judgement, attention and learning, risk assessment and confidence.

I firmly believe that trauma impacts our minds and our cognition so much due to a few very simple reasons. The first is exhaustion (physical and emotional), the second is hypervigilance and safety-seeking, and the third is unpredictability.

Psychological trauma causes a level of exhaustion that is unique. We feel like we are on a horror-ride we cannot get off. Our adrenaline and cortisol are playing havoc with us, and we are at the mercy of our hormones for weeks or months. Our sleep patterns become disturbed, and so all of our natural rhythms are thrown out. If we are in sleep deprivation, cognition will get pretty damn wavy within a few days – and if that sleep deprivation continues, especially if you live on a few hours of broken sleep each day, the impact on our brains and minds is significant.

Because our sleeping and living changes, so does our eating. We eat at weird times, we eat foods that make us feel crap, or we stop eating. Our body is used to releasing and using gut microbes and enzymes at certain times of day, and so, if we stop sleeping, and begin eating at unpredictable times, we are much more likely to have upset stomachs and problems with digestion, because the enzymes and gut microbes we need are out of sync with our new eating patterns.

(If you ever fly long haul, and get an upset stomach, this is why! Jetlag causes you to eat at times when your body isn't ready, and so the enzymes, gut microbes, and digestive patterns are no longer in sync, causing you to feel unwell when you have eaten. The same happens in sleep deprivation!)

Eating is ultimately the way we get fuel for our bodies and brain, so when our eating drops, so does our energy. Our thinking will slow down, we may feel like we have brain fog, feel dizzy, not be able to pay attention or focus, and our memory may be affected.

And exhaustion isn't just physical, it can be a deeply emotional feeling, too. When we have cycled through so many feelings and emotions due to trauma, we can eventually reach a level of burnout which means that we either become numb, or we become extremely sensitive and fragile.

The second reason I mentioned was hypervigilance and safety-seeking. To me, it makes total sense why our cognitive abilities and patterns would change, if we were constantly in survival mode. We very often end up in a hypervigilant state when we have been traumatised, because our body and mind wants to protect us from anything like that happening to us again.

However, this constant scanning, analysing and searching for danger (or searching for safety) will take a toll on the rest of our cognitive tasks.

Are we really going to remember that shopping list if going to the supermarket scares the shit out of us? Are we going to be able to read that book and remember what we just read, if we are subconsciously scanning the environment for risks?

Are we going to be able to focus on work or at school, when we are having endless flashbacks and feelings of danger?

Of course not. Our mind is very busy trying to keep us safe, and other tasks take a back seat. Simply put, they are not a priority. And yet (especially as women), we are expected to continue on with life, remembering every birthday, appointment, shopping list, recipe, chore, school trip, task at work, meeting, and deadline – despite the fact that our brain is very busy working out whether we are in danger of being hurt.

The third cause I mentioned is unpredictability.

Trauma is very often an unpredictable event, and one that shocks you in some way. Maybe you had a car accident, or maybe your partner of twelve years has been abusing your children. Maybe your boss tries to rape you at a Christmas party, or your pregnancy ends in miscarriage just after your exciting 12-week scan.

Trauma slaps us in the face, and teaches us that nothing is promised to us. Nothing is predictable, and everything we thought was safe and steady, might not be anymore.

From a cognitive perspective, this plays havoc with our poor brain, that relies on rules and stereotypes whilst in autopilot. What once was so safe and comfortable, suddenly feels very dangerous and risky.

Every time you get in your car, you may start to worry that you could crash. Every time your kid gets a temperature, you might worry that its meningitis. Every time a man goes to hug you, you might worry that he's going to grab your ass.

This is not you becoming 'paranoid', but is a direct result of your brain realising that trauma can strike at any time, and danger is possible around every corner. In extreme examples of this trauma response, it means some people never leave the house – or even their own bedroom.

However, even though I say 'extreme example', I don't think that becoming terrified of unpredictable danger is an abnormal response at all, I think it is totally normal. Extreme trauma, and extreme danger will elicit extreme responses. There is nothing wrong about that – especially when the trauma has taught us that nowhere is safe.

Bu back to the impact on our mind, we can then begin to understand why the issue of unpredictability will change the way we think, make decisions and risk assess situations. If nothing is predictable, and anything can happen at any time, our mind has to work overtime to figure our what and who is safe, what is happening, what is going to happen next, and what we might need to do. This will of course impact our attention span, our decision making and our judgement.

Next, lets break down each of the impacts on our mind in more detail:

Memories and Flashbacks

Trauma can create a real rollercoaster with your memory. You might find yourself forgetting things, or, on the flip side, experiencing intrusive flashbacks that feel like you're reliving the moment. Flashbacks aren't a sign of weakness or failure; they're your brain's way of trying to process what happened.

Flashbacks can feel scary, but I sometimes wonder if this is because we have given them another name – and in a way – pathologised them. Flashbacks are just memories. They come up for us in the way all memories do: they are triggered by some stimulus. This is exactly the same way all memories work. Maybe when you smell paint, you remember moving into your first house and decorating it. Maybe when you hear a certain song, memories coming flooding back of a summer in the 90s when it was in the charts.

Similarly, you could smell cigarettes and get thrown back to the time when your ex beat you up. Or you could drive through your hometown and remember the moment you got the call to say that your mother had died suddenly.

And what about the boring stuff? We see an advert on TV, and we remember we ran out of toilet paper. We see a woman stood at the side of the road with her broken down car, and remember that we need to book our car in for a service.

Our memories are not inherently good or bad. They just are. There is no such thing as a 'trauma memory', really. Our memories are a part of us, and they are triggered constantly. I do wonder if sometimes, it would be better to learn and think about our memories as more neutral than we currently do when we discuss trauma, especially as people spend so much of their lives hiding from their own memories, repressing them, avoiding them and denying them – whilst wondering why they keep popping up!

On a slightly different note, I have met with many people over the years who talk about the impact of trauma on their memory recall. They often talk about how they feel their memory for basic day-to-day things and tasks has been impacted by how traumatised they are. They forget their keys. They leave cupboards open. They burn their food in the oven. They forget to pay bills. They don't turn up to appointments they booked.

For lots of people, this gradual (or sudden) change in their memory can be frightening and confusing – but it is actually a very common response to trauma.

Fatigue

Trauma can be exhausting - physically, mentally, and emotionally. It's like your body and mind are carrying around this invisible weight. Trauma often keeps the nervous system in overdrive, stuck in fight, flight, or freeze mode, which drains your energy. Even when you're resting, your body might not feel like it's truly recovering. You may notice that no matter how much sleep you get, it is never enough to make you feel well rested, and this will be related to the quality of your sleep and REM cycles. Even when we sleep, if we do not reach deep, restful and regenerative sleep, it is likely that we will wake up feeling pretty terrible.

Fatigue is a natural response to carrying so much, and we often have so many responsibilities and roles in our lives that we don't give ourselves permission to rest.

Decision-Making and Judgement

Have you ever felt like making even the simplest decision is impossible after trauma? You're not alone. Trauma can mess with our reasoning, our confidence in our decisions and our judgement. When the brain is busy managing a trauma response, it's harder to weigh options or think clearly. We may also be influenced by our feelings of fear, anger, risk and danger. Be gentle with yourself if you're second-guessing everything or doubting yourself. It's not about you being indecisive; it's your brain doing its best under pressure.

Attention and Focus

Trauma can make it really hard to concentrate. It's like your brain is stuck in survival mode, constantly scanning for danger, which leaves little room for focus. You might zone out or struggle to stay present. You might feel totally burned out after focussing on something for a short time. You might even notice that your attention span is virtually zero since the trauma. This isn't laziness or lack of effort; it's your mind prioritising safety over everything else. Focus and attention will come back in time - it's okay to take things slowly – and slowing down is the first step to acknowledging and validating yourself here.

If you keep forcing yourself to focus and pay attention to things for long periods of time (such as work or study), whilst still traumatised, you will probably begin to feel extremely tired, demotivated, and might even make mistakes which affect your confidence and self-esteem.

Knowledge Retention and Learning New Things

Learning and remembering new information can feel like climbing a mountain when you're dealing with trauma. This is because the stress hormones released during trauma can make it harder for your brain to store information. Your brain might prioritise survival-related processes over learning. It's not a reflection of your intelligence or capability; it's your brain conserving energy for what it thinks is most urgent.

When we have been in a traumatic situation, our basic survival instincts mean that our brain will be looking for further danger and risk – and whilst this is happening, it is understandable that you are not going to be taking in information and retaining it in the same was as if you were feeling safe and relaxed.

Assessment of Risky Situations

Trauma can skew how we see risk. Some people become hyper-vigilant, seeing danger everywhere, while others might take risks they wouldn't normally take. Both are rooted in trauma - hyper-vigilance comes from a heightened sense of fear, while risk-taking can stem from numbness or a desire to feel in control again. Neither response is your fault, and both are your brain's way of coping with what it's been through.

Confidence

Let's be real: trauma can shatter your confidence. It can make you doubt yourself, your abilities, and even your self-worth. This isn't because you're weak; it's because trauma often involves blame, shame, or feelings of helplessness. Rebuilding confidence after trauma takes time, but it's absolutely possible. The first step to working on this, is to recognise how much of an impact trauma has had on your confidence in your decisions.

I hope this section has helped those of you who have been questioning changes in your thinking and cognitive processes since the trauma. You are not disordered or broken – but you are exhausted and feeling unsafe from the trauma – and it is having an impact on your mind.

If any of this resonates with you, know that you're not broken, and you're not alone. Trauma affects us deeply, but it doesn't define us. Healing is a journey - one that looks different for everyone - and every step you take, no matter how small, is a victory. Be kind to yourself; you're doing the best you can with what you've been through. And that is enough.

How do you feel your trauma affected or influenced your decision making?

How confident are you in the decisions you make in your life since the trauma?

Did fatigue play a role during or since your trauma? How has fatigue showed up for you?

Some people say that they become overly critical of themselves after trauma. Do you think this applies to you? In what way?

Have you noticed any changes in your attention span during or since the trauma? How could this be connected?

How do your trauma memories come up for you? Are they intrusive and random, or are they triggered by specific things?

How has the trauma impacted your ability to retain knowledge and learning? Why do you think this is?

Some people say that trauma impacted their assessment of risky situations and people – either in a way that meant they saw risk when it wasn't there, or in a way which meant they had normalised risk and danger. Does this apply to you?

Are there certain people or situations you are a lot more suspicious or wary of since the trauma?

Do you have any cognitive changes or experiences that you used to think were mental disorders, but now think are connected to the trauma you went through?

Do you feel that you listen to your intuition and inner voice, or ignore it? Why?

When you have had flashbacks or intrusive memories, how have you responded to them? Has this helped or made the experience worse?

How do you feel your judgement of others has changed since the trauma?

How does self-doubt show up in your life since the trauma? Is this something you need to explore more?

Have any cognitive impacts from trauma been mistaken for medical issues or mental disorders?

Way to go! You completed the fifth step, 'The impact of trauma on my mind'. An interesting section!

Write one thing you learned about yourself from this step.

Write one thing that challenged you to think differently in this step.

Use this space to encourage yourself to work through this programme. Tell yourself how well you are doing!

Step 6: The impact of trauma on my body

Welcome to the sixth step of *The Amethyst Programme*!

You're almost halfway through!

This step builds on the previous, by looking at the impact trauma has had on our bodies, our health and illnesses.

When we talk about the impact of trauma, we often focus on emotions and mental health, but the truth is, trauma can manifest physically in ways that are just as significant. It can feel like your body is failing you, or breaking down. It's your body trying to cope with overwhelming stress, often long after the trauma itself has passed – which is due to the way cortisol acts on the body over months and years.

This step is especially for those of you who are struggling with your physical health since the trauma, and those of you who have received no support, no understanding and no validation about how much your body has suffered.

When you experience trauma, your nervous system goes into survival mode, we know this, we have discussed this already. This is essential during the traumatic event itself, but if your nervous system stays stuck in that heightened state, it starts to take a toll on your physical health.

Your body becomes flooded with stress hormones like cortisol and adrenaline, which are great for short bursts of survival but harmful when they linger. Over time, this chronic activation can lead to wear and tear on your organs and systems.

One common way trauma manifests is through chronic inflammation. When your body is in a constant state of alert, it can't properly regulate its immune response. This can trigger inflammatory conditions like arthritis, IBS, or even heart disease.

For example, someone who has survived repeated trauma might develop an autoimmune condition, where the body mistakenly attacks its own tissues. This is a valid and real physiological response to prolonged stress.

Trauma also affects the gut. You've probably felt 'butterflies' in your stomach when you're nervous – that's your gut and brain communicating. Trauma disrupts this connection, often causing irritable bowel syndrome (IBS) or other digestive issues. For instance, someone who's experienced childhood trauma might notice chronic stomach pain or bloating, even when there's no obvious medical cause. Many tests later, and many appointments later, you are no closer to knowing what is 'wrong' with your stomach – and that's because there is nothing medically wrong. This is your body expressing what words sometimes can't.

Another way trauma shows up is in chronic pain. Even if there's no identifiable injury, people with trauma histories often report pain in their neck, back, or joints. This can be linked to muscle tension – your body literally holding onto stress – or to the way trauma changes how your brain processes pain signals. For example, if you've been through a physically threatening experience, your brain might stay hypervigilant, interpreting even minor sensations as pain.

Trauma impacts sleep, which plays a critical role in physical health. Poor sleep from trauma-related nightmares or hyperarousal can weaken your immune system, disrupt hormone balance, and make existing conditions worse. It's a vicious cycle: the less you sleep, the more your body struggles to recover, and the more your trauma responses intensify.

Even conditions like high blood pressure, migraines, skin issues, stroke, and heart disease can have roots in unresolved trauma. For example, someone who's lived with constant stress from an unsafe environment might develop hypertension because their body has spent years bracing for danger.

The role of cortisol

Cortisol and adrenaline are hormones produced by the adrenal glands in response to stress. These hormones play a crucial role in the body's 'fight or flight' response, which is a natural response to a perceived threat. When the body is under stress, cortisol and adrenaline are released into the bloodstream, which triggers several physiological changes, including:

• Increased heart rate and blood pressure

• Increased respiration rate

• Dilated pupils

• Increased blood sugar levels

• Suppressed immune system response

While the distress response is designed to be helpful in short-term situations, chronic distress can cause ongoing health problems. For example, high levels of cortisol and adrenaline over time can lead to:

• High blood pressure

• Increased risk of heart disease

• Impaired immune system function

• Increased risk of infection

• Impaired memory and concentration

• Fatigue

• Sleep problems

Health issues related to trauma

This section has been adapted from our huge A-Z of trauma responses and coping mechanisms, 'The Indicative Trauma Impact Manual', written by myself and my wife, Jaimi Shrive, in 2023.

Here are some examples of health issues that can be caused or worsened by trauma. This list is not exhaustive, and only represents a tiny fraction of possible health issues related to trauma.

Acne	Headaches	Sleep disturbance
Bedwetting	Hyperventilating	Stomach pain
Blurred vision	IBS	Sweating
Body aches	Inability to orgasm	Throat tightness
Chest pain	Inability to yawn	Thrush
Daydreaming	Insomnia	Thyroid issues
Dizziness	Irregular periods	UTIs
Echoey hearing	Muscle spasms	Tics and twitching
Fainting	Nerve pain	Tinnitus
Food changes	Palpitations	Vaginismus
Hair loss	Shakes and tremors	Vitamin deficiency

As can be seen from the lists above, the impact on our body can be global and significant, and what makes this worse, is that we rarely connect the dots back to the psychological trauma and distress.

For me, as an example, my most common ones off that list when I am traumatised are blurred vision (which used to terrify me!), chest pain, (also used to terrify me… many a day spent up A&E with that one), dizziness (horrible), fainting (would not recommend), hair loss (worrying but manageable), headaches (I should have shares in paracetamol), and irregular periods (although, thanks to the trauma of the past few years, I have unfortunately gone into ovary insufficiency, where my periods and my ovaries have stopped working – which causes a very early menopause, which is enormous fun at 34).

As you can probably imagine, that combination of symptoms, plus my weight fluctuations – is enough to send any of us running to a doctor. It has taken me years of patience, self-education and exploration to understand that my body is not dying of some mystery syndrome, but it is expressing years of trauma and burnout. Where once I was the person turning up at hospital and my doctor every few weeks with a new mystery health complaint, I slowly learned that there was nothing physically wrong with me, but the impact of cortisol was playing holy hell with my body.

I realised that the only real way for those health issues to improve would be to process the trauma, dramatically reduce stress in my life, pack up my shit and live on a deserted island for a few years.

I'm only half joking! Don't worry, I am not about to move to a desert island… unless you have one? In that case, email me.

But seriously, this understanding of my body and my health changed my life. I was so scared of my own bodily responses to my trauma that I was worsening and heightening my own responses. I realised, for example, that when I felt dizzy from my cortisol levels rising, I would get really frightened of the dizziness, and then become even more stressed, releasing even more cortisol, worsening the dizzy spells, and causing me all sorts of problems.

However, when I stopped reacting to the dizziness, and instead stayed deliberately calm and told myself it was related to cortisol levels changing, and that I needed to rest, the dizziness would go away after ten minutes or so, and I could get on with my day.

I experienced the exact same improvement with my chest pains. I would get chest tightness from panic attacks, convince myself I was having a heart attack, end up absolutely petrified, increase the tightness of my chest and the pains, and then eventually end up so scared I would pass out or faint. But when I realised what I was doing and stopped reacting to the chest pain, I stopped the cycle of fear and pain.

It genuinely changed my life, just by understanding my health issues more deeply, and how they were connected to trauma – and I wished that someone had taught me this much earlier!

List all of the impacts the trauma has had on your body and your health

What has been the biggest impact on your body or your health since the trauma?

Which of your health issues have you later realised are connected to your trauma?

Consider your menstrual cycle, your menopause, or your fertility. How do you feel the trauma impacted you?

During and after the trauma, did you notice any changes to your hair, nails or skin?

What happened to your sleeping patterns during and after the trauma? Did you begin to sleep more, less, or experience broken sleep?

Describe how you think, feel and behave when you are sleep deprived from the trauma. How many of these impacts have you mistaken for 'mental health' issues?

What was the impact of the trauma on your heart health, blood pressure and heartrate? Did you experience palpitations or chest pains? What did you think they were at the time?

Consider your digestive system. How do you think trauma has impacted or changed your digestion?

What impact did the trauma have on your appetite and eating habits?

Write about the impact of any injuries or scars you have from trauma. Do you still have them? How do they impact you?

Consider the holistic impact of the trauma on your health. Did you notice an impact on your immune system at all?

Have you ever sought help for health issues that you now realise were connected to your trauma? How were you treated?

Way to go! You completed the sixth step, 'The impact of trauma on my body'. You're halfway through!

Write one thing you learned about yourself from this step.

Write one thing that challenged you to think differently in this step.

Use this space to congratulate yourself for getting halfway through this programme. Congratulations!

Step 7: The impact of trauma on my spirit

Welcome to the seventh step of *The Amethyst Programme*.

We have talked about our bodies, we have talked about our minds – but what about something deeper? Something a little more elusive?

Exploring spirituality and connecting to a sense of higher consciousness after trauma and abuse can be a deeply healing journey. Trauma often leaves us feeling disconnected - disconnected from ourselves, from others, and from a sense of meaning or purpose. Spirituality, in whatever form resonates with you, offers a way to reconnect and to make sense of experiences that can otherwise feel overwhelming or senseless. It's not about subscribing to a particular belief system, but about finding practices and perspectives that bring comfort, clarity, and a deeper sense of connection.

Connecting with and exploring spirituality is different for everyone.

For me, reconnecting with 'spirituality' has been about the following:

• Realising that I have been looking for purpose, meaning and explanations in my life that have never been fulfilled – before, during or after trauma

• Getting comfortable with the fact that we have absolutely no evidence of what 'consciousness' is, how it is produced by the brain, and how to 'measure' or 'test' it – and therefore, I should be much more open to what the mind and brain is capable of

• Accepting that I have had hundreds of weird and spiritual experiences ranging from hearing messages through to deep gut instincts about someone that cannot be explained by current science, and that is okay!

• Noticing that when I get into a meditative state, I see and hear things that I am not able to access when I am fully alert and awake – and in lots of cases, these visions and messages have been helpful, transformative, challenging and interesting

• Being open to alternative explanations of consciousness, soul, spirit, life, death, dreams, intuition and our connection to the universe – without shutting them down as 'stupid' or 'hippy bullshit' or 'unscientific' (which I always used to do!)

• Being comfortable with the fact that we know very little about our universe, about our world, and even less about how our brain works – so why rule anything out?

• Being highly critical of traditional and modern psychiatry and psychology, which has meant that I have rejected many of the dominant theories which suggest that consciousness is a meaningless byproduct of biological function, and dreams are nothing more than mixed up memory processing. This has impacted my theories and my explanations of trauma and anti-pathology, since both psychiatry and psychology seeks to frame us as mentally ill after trauma – which I reject.

• Having deeply challenging experiences during sound baths and meditation sessions around the world, which have changed the way I think about our mind and body, but have also significantly helped me and others process trauma.

• Recognising that our history of British colonialism has deliberately destroyed indigenous and ancient ways of connecting to the body and mind, and all the wisdom, knowledge and skill that went with that – and were forcibly replaced with Christianity, capitalism and imperialism

• Understanding that we have much to learn, and our current approaches to trauma and the human condition are causing mass harm to the global population, which others are profiting from

• Exploring whether we are being kept in a state of fear, distress and trauma by governments and those in power, because we are easier to control and manipulate when we are scared, divided and confused.

Anyway – I have been on my own journey into the depths of myself after many years of ignoring and repressing those depths – and I wanted to provide a space for you to do the same. You don't have to believe in any of it to learn about it – and if none of this resonates with you, that's absolutely okay.

If I had read this a few years ago, I would have skipped past!

So, let's go back to basics.

Trauma disrupts everything - our sense of safety, our identity, and often our belief in the goodness and purpose of the world. After trauma, it's common to feel untethered, as though the foundation you stood on has been shaken. You might find yourself questioning everything: Why did this happen? What does it mean? Where do I go from here? What is the point of any of this? Will I suffer endlessly for no reason? Why me?

These questions can feel heavy, even unbearable, especially if the trauma has left you feeling isolated or unsupported.

Spirituality offers a way to hold these questions, not by giving definitive answers (in the way a religion does) but by creating space for exploration.

Spirituality is very different from religion, and so, even though spirituality is a big part of my life now, I still don't believe in any organised religions. What I do believe though, is that we are likely to be a small part of something much larger, and just because we don't understand it, doesn't mean it isn't there. I often remind myself that much of our technology today would have been written off as witchcraft, demons, and magic only 100 years ago.

Spirituality can provide a framework for understanding your pain, not as something random or meaningless but as part of a larger journey. This isn't about justifying what happened - trauma is never deserved - but about finding ways to process and grow from it.

For me, I have never used spirituality to go down the path of 'law of attraction' and 'you get back what you put out' – because I think this totally ignores free will of others who wish to cause harm. I don't believe that everything happens for a reason, due to the same logic around free will. Some things happen to us because someone else made a decision that affects us. However, I have used spirituality to find meaning in my own thoughts, responses, ideas, feelings and confusion.

What is spirituality?

Spirituality is deeply personal, and it doesn't have to involve religion or traditional beliefs. For some, it's about connecting with nature, meditating, or finding solace in the rhythms of the universe. The moon cycles wax and wane. The sun rises and sets. The seasons move along. The tides go in and out, controlled by the moon. Our bodies respond to all of these natural rhythms, and yet, we are so cut off from them all. My first steps into spirituality were probably through my interest in astronomy and stargazing.

I have spent countless nights lay under the stars somewhere, watching the sky move and breathe, wondering what we are and why we are here.

For others, it might mean exploring the teachings of spiritual leaders, philosophers, connecting with ancestors, or simply cultivating a sense of awe and wonder. At its core, spirituality is about seeking meaning, connection, and a sense of belonging to something greater than yourself.

After trauma, spirituality can help you reconnect with that 'something greater,' whether it's the vastness of the cosmos, the power of love and kindness, a higher version of your own consciousness or mind, an energy you tap into, your connection to the earth or nature, or a broader higher power you believe in. It can remind you that you are not alone in your pain and that your life has value and purpose beyond what you've endured.

How Spirituality Helps Process Trauma

Trauma can often feel senseless, leaving you questioning why it happened or what it means. While spirituality doesn't erase the pain, it can offer ways to reframe your experiences. For example, some people find solace in viewing their struggles as part of a larger journey toward growth or understanding. This doesn't mean the trauma was 'meant to be' or that it happened for a reason - it's about choosing to find meaning in how you move forward.

I have never looked back on my own abuse and rapes and thought, 'Well, it must have all happened for a reason! Look where I am today!'

For me, that's too far into toxic positivity and victim blaming. I would sooner have never been beaten up, abused or raped. End of story.

But what I have used it for, is to understand how I am supposed to keep plodding on every day when I have never received any justice. How and why I am who I am. Why I feel this deep need to educate others. Why I push so hard when I have nothing left in the tank. Why I live such a principled life (even to my own detriment). Why I am obsessed with right and wrong. Why I tell the truth even when I am hated for it. Why I feel people should have the power to work through their own trauma without interference from the state. Why I am drawn to strange and difficult experiences, and why they keep happening to me. Why we see religion as a belief system, but not psychiatry.

Meditation, sound baths and journalling have all helped me answer some of my deepest questions – and have allowed me to access some of my most vulnerable and repressed places. Not only this, but I have found solace, strength, and inspiration when I have felt totally alone, and totally exhausted.

Spirituality also invites you to consider that your pain doesn't define you – which is something I had been saying for years as a trauma-informed psychologist. Instead, it's one chapter in a much larger story - one that includes resilience, love, and transformation.

Trauma often leaves you feeling disconnected from your body, your emotions, and your sense of self. Spiritual practices like meditation, breathwork, trauma release exercises, or prayer can help you tune back into your inner world and listen to yourself. They create moments of stillness where you can listen to your intuition, honour your feelings, and reconnect with the parts of yourself that feel whole, solid and unbroken.

For some, this might mean sitting quietly in nature and noticing how your body feels in the presence of something larger than yourself. Sit at the base of a tree. Feel your skin on the grass. Dig your bare feet into the sand. Swim in freshwater lakes, or float in the sea. For others, it could involve journalling or creative expression as a way to explore your inner thoughts and emotions.

Spirituality often emphasises compassion - both for yourself and for others. After trauma, it's common to carry feelings of shame, guilt, blame, or anger. Spirituality can help you soften these feelings by reminding you that you are not your pain, you are not defined by your trauma, or your mistakes. You are a complex, imperfect human being deserving of love and understanding. You are capable of growth and total change.

Forgiveness can also be a part of this process, though it's important to note that forgiveness doesn't mean excusing what happened or reconciling with those who hurt you. It's about freeing yourself from the weight of resentment and reclaiming your energy for your own healing. However, I do often teach that forgiveness is not required for you to move on, and I don't agree with the teachings which state that you must forgive as part of trauma processing.

Trauma isolates us, making us feel alone in our pain. Spirituality reminds us that we are part of something larger - a community, a lineage, a culture, an energy, a collective, an earth, a universe. Whether it's through shared rituals, moments of collective prayer, or simply recognising the interconnectedness of all living things, spirituality can help you feel less alone.

For example, many find healing in connecting with nature, recognising that just as the seasons change and the earth regenerates, they too have the capacity to grow and heal.

Higher consciousness doesn't have to be a mystical or complicated concept - it's simply the idea of expanding your awareness beyond the immediate pain of your trauma. Through practices like meditation, yoga, reiki, sound baths, or mindfulness, you can cultivate a sense of presence and peace that transcends the chaos of your thoughts. This doesn't mean avoiding your pain; it means learning to hold it with grace and perspective.

Higher consciousness invites you to see yourself not just as a survivor, or as someone who is 'broken', but as a whole, evolving being with the capacity for joy, love, and transformation.

Which of your beliefs have changed the most since the trauma?

If you have ever had a faith or religion, how would the teachings and beliefs explain your trauma? Do you find this helpful or harmful?

Some people say that every experience can teach us something about ourselves or others. What do you think about that in relation to your own trauma?

What did the traumatic experience force you to confront, that
you had been avoiding or ignoring?

How have your traumatic experiences changed the way you
see the world?

Has the trauma you have been through changed your connection to spirituality?

How do you feel your trauma has influenced your thoughts
about the meaning of life?

Do you think your beliefs or ideas have evolved through the trauma? What has changed?

How do you feel when people say, 'what doesn't kill you makes you stronger'?

Has the trauma forced you to question anything you thought you 'knew'? What have you questioned, and how do you feel about it now?

How has your purpose or role in life changed since the trauma?

Do you feel the trauma has made you more open-minded, or less open-minded? Why do you feel this?

Some people say that everything happens for a reason – how do you feel about this saying in relation to your own trauma?

Have you ever experienced something spiritual or
paranormal? How did you feel about it?

Is there anything that you used to reject or disagree with, that you now accept or agree with, due to the impact or influence of the trauma on your life?

Way to go! You completed the seventh step, 'The impact of trauma on my spirit'. How has that left you feeling?

Write one thing you learned about yourself from this step.

Write one thing that challenged you to think differently in this step.

Use this space to encourage yourself to work through this programme. Tell yourself how well you are doing!

Step 8: Challenging pathologisation and self-blame

Wow! You're doing brilliantly. Step eight, already!

Well done for getting this far through the programme. The last step is fascinating!

In this step, we are going to work on our pathologisation and our self-blame.

Let's start with blame, and then move on to pathologisation later.

By far, one of the most damaging experiences we can go through, is to be blamed for being abused and harmed by others. In fact, many people say that being blamed is worse than the abuse itself.

My own experience of this has been myriad.

When I was raped and abused as a teenager, I was blamed by my friends, and my mum. When I was beaten up and my shoulder was dislocated at 18 years old, I was blamed by the police and told I was wasting their time. When I was attacked and hospitalised back in 2012 and had to have stitches in my face and mouth, the police blamed me – and suggested the total stranger (who had appeared from behind me and had knocked me unconscious with a knuckle duster as I turned around) must have acted in self-defence. When a man sexually assaulted me in a bar at 25 years old, I had told him I didn't want a drink with him; I was blamed by the bouncer and told I was ruining the man's birthday.

When my holiday photos were stolen and used on a fake account to defraud men a few years ago, I was blamed by my feminist colleagues for posting them in the first place.

When I was being stalked and harassed recently, I was blamed by police for 'going looking for the evidence', even though they told me to collect evidence in order to make the arrest.

The list goes on. And it does for most of us.

It is common, for example, to blame children who are being bullied at school. Frequently, the response from teachers and parents is, 'But what did you do to provoke them? You must have said or done something to make them do this? Why didn't you tell a teacher? Why didn't you tell them to fuck off? Why don't you just stay away from them?'

When women are catcalled in the street, or sexually harassed in a bar, the victim blaming kicks in almost instantly. 'But what signals were you giving off? Why didn't you just tell him you weren't interested? What were you wearing? Did you flirt with him? How much had you had to drink?'

We are very likely to be subjected to blaming and shaming from others – whether we are in a hospital with an illness, at a family gathering talking about being bullied in the workplace, or in a police station giving a statement.

In my work, particularly in my 2020 book, *Why Women Are Blamed for Everything'*, I've spent a lot of time examining why we, as individuals, and we as a society, blame victims of abuse and trauma instead of supporting them or holding perpetrators and oppressive systems accountable.

It's something I've seen time and time again – whether it's in my research, my practice, the media, or the stories shared with me by survivors. The truth is, victim-blaming isn't just harmful; it's deeply ingrained in the way we're taught to view trauma, responsibility, and control.

One of the key reasons we blame victims is that it's easier for people to focus on what the victim did or didn't do than to face the uncomfortable reality that abuse and trauma can happen to anyone.

Blaming the victim creates a false sense of security – the idea that if we just follow certain rules or avoid certain behaviours, we can prevent harm.

For example, when someone says, "Why did she stay in the relationship?" or "Why was she walking alone at night?" what they're really doing is distancing themselves from the fear that it could happen to them. It's a coping mechanism – one that protects their sense of safety but deeply harms survivors.

I see this reaction a lot – from everyone really, but especially from professionals. It bothers me to hear it from a member of the public, but it deeply troubles me when I hear a social worker, a psychologist, therapist, police officer, teacher, nurse or psychiatrist use this reasoning about any form of harm to another person.

Very often, professionals believe that due to their extensive training, their views are better, more educated, and more moral than those of the lay public – but I have never found this to be the case. They often engage in victim blaming and announce that they would never (insert action here) – and therefore, they would never be put in the same situation or trauma as their client or patient. This always results in one of my epic and totally uncontrollable eye rolls.

But it goes beyond individual psychology. Victim-blaming is also systemic.

It's baked into the very structures that are supposed to protect us. Women, in particular, are often labelled as "hysterical" or "mentally unstable" when they speak out about abuse, while perpetrators are excused with phrases like, "He's such a good guy" or "He didn't mean it." These narratives aren't accidental – they're designed to protect abusers and maintain the status quo. If survivors are silenced or discredited, the systems that allow abuse to thrive remain unchallenged.

It's not just abuse or violence that we blame people for, though. In my work, I've seen how we also blame people for other forms of trauma that don't have a clear perpetrator – like illnesses, accidents, or natural disasters. Someone diagnosed with a chronic illness might hear, "You should have eaten better", or "You didn't exercise enough," as if their suffering is the result of their own choices.

When someone is injured in an accident, they might be told, "You should have been more careful", or "Why didn't you see it coming?" Even survivors of disasters like floods or fires are often met with questions like, "Why didn't you leave sooner?", or "Why didn't you prepare?"

These forms of victim-blaming stem from the same discomfort with vulnerability and unpredictability. As a society, we cling to the belief that bad things only happen to people who "deserve" them, because the alternative – that trauma and devastation can strike anyone, anywhere, at any time – is too terrifying for many to face. Blaming the victim allows people to maintain the illusion that the world is fair, and that they have control over their own fate.

This tendency to blame isn't just about individuals, though; it's reinforced by systems of oppression like patriarchy, racism, classism, and ableism. These systems teach us to view trauma and hardship as personal failings rather than as the result of systemic issues or random events. If we believe that illness is caused by poor lifestyle choices or that accidents happen because someone wasn't 'careful enough,' we don't have to confront the broader societal and systemic factors at play. It's easier to blame individuals than to question the systems that perpetuate harm.

The impact of this blame on survivors is devastating. It compounds their trauma, isolates them from support, and often silences them altogether. Survivors begin to internalise these messages, asking themselves, "Was it my fault? Could I have done something differently?" This self-blame is corrosive, making it harder for people to heal and move forward.

In my work, I focus on challenging these narratives. I believe it's crucial to reframe how we view trauma and responsibility.

Instead of asking, "Why did this person let this happen?" we need to ask, "Why did this happen to them? Why did someone do this to them? Why do our systems allow this to happen? Why is there no justice or protection? How can we prevent it in the future?"

The responsibility for harm – whether it's abuse, illness, crime, natural disaster, or an accident – doesn't lie with the person who experienced it. It lies with those who caused it or, in cases without a clear perpetrator, with the broader systems and structures that failed to protect them or support them afterwards.

Ultimately, we need to dismantle the culture of victim-blaming and replace it with one of compassion, understanding, and accountability.

Blaming people for their trauma – whether it's abuse, illness, or misfortune – doesn't make the world any safer for anyone. It just perpetuates harm.

True change comes when we hold systems and perpetrators accountable, support survivors without judgment, and acknowledge that trauma is not a personal failing but a reflection of larger forces at play. Only then can we begin to build a society where survivors are seen, heard, and valued for the incredible strength it takes to endure and overcome.

Victim-blaming in abuse and trauma isn't just an unfortunate by-product of ignorance or lack of compassion, either. It serves specific functions that benefit individuals, communities, and systems of power.

It's a way to deflect responsibility, maintain control, and protect the status quo. While it deeply harms victims and survivors, it offers a sense of comfort and protection to everyone else – individuals, communities, and those in power. It is important to understand who benefits from victim blaming. Let's break it down.

For individuals who haven't experienced abuse or trauma, victim-blaming provides an illusion of safety and control in their lives and in their environments. By blaming the victim, people can convince themselves that the harm was a result of the victim's actions or choices: They should've left earlier, they shouldn't have worn that, or they were too trusting. These narratives create a mental barrier between the observer and the reality of trauma. It allows them to believe that they can avoid similar harm by simply 'doing the right things' or making 'better' choices.

The alternative – recognising that harm often happens unpredictably and unjustly, and that anyone can become a victim – is terrifying. Acknowledging that trauma could happen to anyone, at any time, forces people to confront their own vulnerability, which is deeply uncomfortable. Victim-blaming offers a way to distance themselves from that discomfort, creating a false sense of control over their own safety.

Communities often lean on victim-blaming to preserve their collective identity and sense of harmony. If harm or abuse occurs within a group – a family, a workplace, a neighbourhood, or even a religious or cultural community – blaming the victim allows the community to avoid accountability, and maintain power. Instead of examining how their own dynamics, values, or inaction might have contributed to the harm, they focus on the victim: 'What did they do to bring this on?' or 'Why didn't they speak up sooner?'

By framing the issue as a personal failure rather than a communal one, the group avoids difficult conversations about its own role in enabling or ignoring harm. For example, in a workplace where harassment occurs, blaming the victim shifts the focus away from systemic issues like toxic culture or inadequate policies. Similarly, in families, victim-blaming helps maintain the illusion of a "good family" while sidelining the person who dared to disrupt the narrative by speaking out.

Victim-blaming also reinforces conformity within the group. Survivors are often scapegoated or ostracised, sending a clear message: Don't challenge the system, don't speak out, and don't disrupt the peace, or you'll face the same blame and isolation. This silences others who might otherwise come forward, ensuring that the group's reputation remains intact.

At its core, victim-blaming is a tool of oppressive systems – patriarchy, racism, classism, ableism, and many more. These systems thrive by maintaining power imbalances, and victim-blaming plays a crucial role in achieving that. Where there are power imbalances, there is always victim blaming.

When abuse or trauma occurs, shifting the blame onto the victim protects the perpetrators and the structures that enable them.

Victim-blaming also keeps people from questioning systemic failures. If someone living in poverty experiences health issues, they're often blamed for their lifestyle choices: They should've eaten healthier, or they shouldn't have had kids if they couldn't afford them. This narrative distracts from systemic issues like lack of access to healthcare, education, or fair wages. By framing trauma as an individual failing, systems of power avoid scrutiny and remain unchallenged.

Even when the harm isn't caused by a single perpetrator, victim-blaming benefits those in power by maintaining existing hierarchies. For example, when communities blame victims of natural disasters for not preparing enough, it deflects attention from the failures of governments or corporations to provide adequate infrastructure or warning systems. The responsibility shifts from the powerful to the powerless, ensuring that systems of inequality remain intact.

Pathologisation

Building on everything I have said here about self-blame and victim blaming, lets now focus on the specific form of blame and labelling called 'pathologisation'.

I started writing and talking about this many years ago, but specifically when I realised that all the women and girls I was working with in a sexual violence service, were all being told by the same team of psychiatric nurses that they all seemed to have developed borderline personality disorder. Literally hundreds of them.

At the time, I had believed everything I had read about mental disorders, but even then, I found it strange that so many women and girls who had all recently disclosed rape and abuse, were being told they all had a personality disorder.

I decided one night to read through all of their case files one by one, looking for patterns and clues. As I read, I realised they were being labelled by professionals who saw them as attention seekers, liars, wastes of resources, exaggerators, trouble causers and promiscuous.

One professional actually joked to me that she wished her client would stop threatening suicide and just kill herself, so she didn't have to support her anymore. I couldn't even breathe, let alone speak. The shock of her coldness towards a young woman who had recently been raped tore through me, and it was then, that I realised that psychiatric labels were tools of control and oppression – they were nothing to do with science or medicine.

For many years, I studied psychiatry, mental health, the history of mental disorders, the evidence base for treatments and medications, and the profit in the pharmaceutical industry. I wrote my first Sunday Times Bestseller, 'Sexy But Psycho', which looks at the deliberate sexualisation and exploitation of women and girls, and then the strategic framing of them as mentally ill whenever they speak out about abuse, harm or trauma.

I realised that there were overlapping benefits of framing women and girls as mentally ill, and blaming them for being abused or traumatised, and I started teaching thousands of professionals about this overlap, and how it affects women and girls around the world.

Pathologisation means to characterise a behaviour, thought or feeling as medically or psychologically abnormal. This includes the practice of seeing those behaviours or thoughts as medical symptoms as an indicator of a disease or disorder of the mind, instead of seeing them as normal and natural.

Pathologisation can be a deliberate act to reframe natural and normal trauma responses and coping mechanisms as abnormal, mental illnesses, disorders, insanity, delusions, attention seeking, and hysteria.

However, pathologisation can also be non-deliberate, by those who truly believe that labelling and 'diagnosing' people with a mental disorder will help them access support and feel better.

It is common for those who have been abused and harmed to be positioned as mentally ill, or for others to suggest that their recall of the abuse is wrong, or impacted by their mental health (or medication).

Pathologisation is often utilised by abusive partners and ex-partners, by systems of power, by society, police, legal services, social services and health services.

Here is a table Jaimi and I developed to use in teaching professionals about the overlap in actions in victim blaming and pathologisation. It may help you to see these patterns in your own life.

VB = Victim blaming   **P** = Pathologisation

Actions	VB	P
Discredits the person as unreliable or not telling the truth	x	x
Makes the person question their experiences	x	x
Positions the person as the cause of their own problems	x	x
Forces the person to look at 'what they did wrong'	x	x
Used to excuse behaviours of perpetrators	x	x
Reduces chances of justice for victims	x	x
Utilises myths, taboo and stereotyping	x	x

As you can see from this handy table, victim blaming and pathologisation have a lot in common – in fact, they work from the same script, and often achieve the same outcomes!

Whether we have been blamed for the trauma, or we have been framed as mentally ill, we can be easily discredited, positioned as the problem, and forced to look at ourselves – instead of ever being validated or protected.

I have written about this process at length in 'Sexy But Psycho', and in 'The Watcher of Your Own Flame', but there are many reasons why and how we are pathologised.

When I teach about trauma, I argue that physiological and psychological trauma is always:

Rational – trauma responses are often repackaged as the irrational behaviours, thoughts and feelings of a mentally ill person, and yet, when we look honestly at whatever 'symptom' has brought a person to the doctor's office, we can usually find a rational response to trauma. I worked with a woman who was diagnosed with several mental health issues which surrounded her 'irrational' responses to the breeze. If she felt a breeze, draught or wind on her face, she would experience very distressing trauma responses.

After years of being medicated and labelled, I had only been speaking to her for two hours when we happened to dig into why the breeze scared her so much. Initially she couldn't tell me why. She said she had no idea why she had such an 'irrational' trigger. She said she had always been told it was part of her mental health issues. I assured her that everything has a root and that all trauma responses had a purpose. Then suddenly she mumbled something about an accident she had decades ago and before shaking her head and quickly dismissing it as irrelevant.

I encouraged her to talk about whatever it was, and she told me that she had had a fall from a great height when she was younger and the last thing she remembered before hitting the floor and breaking her spine was the rush of the air on her face. Her trigger was wholly rational. Sometimes, trauma responses and coping mechanisms seem irrational because they are out of context, but generally, patience and compassion will always reveal the root and rational cause.

Normal – when a woman or girl has been through something life threatening, terrifying, deeply upsetting or violating, isn't it completely normal that it would impact her for many years to come? The study of mental illness was originally (and up until very recently in many universities and books), called 'abnormal psychology'. The question here is why we have ever considered trauma and distress of humans to be 'abnormal' at all. If a girl is abused or traumatised, wouldn't it be completely normal for her to be affected by that? Wouldn't her nightmares or fears or anger be totally normal? Wouldn't it be abnormal for her not to be affected?

Psychiatry relies on the framing of normal trauma responses as abnormal or disordered thinking and behaviour. Trauma -informed and anti-pathology approaches (like this programme!) consider that our 'symptoms' and 'signs' are completely normal responses to distress and trauma, rather than medicalising or pathologising them.

Natural – many of our trauma responses and coping mechanisms are natural physical and psychological responses to something that has deeply affected us. Whether it's a chronic fear of something happening to us through to physiological reactions such as high heart rate, dizziness, headaches or digestive issues, the causes of these responses are natural processes that have a purpose. They do not constitute medical or mental illnesses. Understanding what our body or mind is trying to do to protect us or to cope is of vital importance to an anti-pathology, trauma -informed approach.

Proportionate – one of the ways that women have been successfully pathologised by psychiatry and mental health movements is by arguing that their responses to trauma or distress are not justified or proportionate. For example, when I ask why grief is now classified as a psychiatric disorder, people say to me, 'Well, it's normal to grieve for a while and for it to impact you, but when it goes on too long or impacts you too much, that's when it becomes a psychiatric disorder.' I often wonder if those people have ever grieved, because my understanding of grief is that it never really goes away.

It's the same with trauma responses and coping mechanisms. If a woman or girl has been abused or harmed for years, wouldn't it be proportionate for her to struggle with that for many years, maybe even her entire life? Why would we think that there would come a day where she would wake up and it would all be fine? Like nothing ever happened.

Trauma responses are almost always proportionate, in my opinion. Women are oppressed globally, subjected to violence and abuse, harassment and discrimination, gender roles and heteronormative pressures to be the perfect woman for men – and this is without individual events of crisis, trauma, illnesses, accidents, bullying, divorce, family breakdown, attacks, injuries, rape, trafficking, exploitation, poverty, homelessness, persecution, natural disasters, and war.

Being frightened, angry, upset, confused, irritable, tired, frustrated or struggling with negative impacts of all of these stressors – for months, years or entire lifetimes – do not justify a label of a mental disorder. They are all proportionate responses to a very difficult way to live as a woman or girl in a patriarchy.

Explainable – one final thing that I try to make clear when teaching about trauma is that all trauma responses and coping mechanisms are explainable. There are no deep dark secrets, no magical or satanic reasons, no dangerous brain chemistries or hidden genes waiting to be unlocked. If someone has developed a coping mechanism or trauma response, there will always be a reason for it, and often, it's a simple one. Rather than listing 'symptoms' of some obscure underlying psychiatric disorder, or chemical imbalance, exploring and explaining the reasons and causes for a change in behaviour, thinking or feeling (no matter how extreme it may seem) is usually fairly simple.

The beauty of this simplicity is that it is also absolutely life changing to realise that you are not to blame, you are not mentally ill, and you deserve support and love whilst you process the trauma.

How do you feel victim blaming has impacted your own life?

Have there been times when you have thought of yourself as 'going crazy' when you have been struggling with your trauma?

Which parts of your trauma have you blamed yourself for and why?

Which of your trauma responses and coping mechanisms have been mistaken for a mental health issue? What was the impact of this?

Who benefits from you thinking your natural trauma responses are actually a mental disorder?

Think about the traumatic experiences you have been through. Can you list three ways in which you have blamed your own behaviour, and three ways in which you have blamed your own character or personality?

Can you think of a time when you have thought your trauma responses or coping mechanisms were abnormal? When did you realise that they were normal and natural feelings and experiences?

Write about a time when you disclosed your trauma or distress to someone, and they suggested you had a mental disorder. Did you believe they were right?

Do you believe you have ever been deliberately pathologised by someone who wanted to frame you as mentally ill? What happened?

Where do you feel you are in your personal journey away from pathologising yourself and your trauma responses?

Who around you totally validates your trauma, and who around you pathologises and gaslights you?

Isn't telling you that your trauma is a 'mental disorder' just another way of silencing and blaming you? How do you feel about this in relation to your own experiences?

Way to go! You completed the eighth step, 'Challenging pathologisation and self-blame'. How are you feeling?

Write one thing you learned about yourself from this step.

Write one thing that challenged you to think differently in this step.

Use this space to encourage yourself to work through this programme. Tell yourself how well you are doing!

Step 9: Validating myself and my experiences

Look at you go! Step nine is here, and we are ready!

You've already worked through so much, so make sure to flick back through your answers as you develop and evolve through the programme.

Our next step is to understand our own connection to validation. Do we feel validated? Did someone validate our feelings and experiences? Did we have to do it all ourselves? And why do we keep seeking validation from that person who doesn't give a shit about us?

Let's get into it.

Lots of us begin to seek validation and acknowledgment after we have been through trauma. To some extent, I think everyone has been here in one way or another.

Seeking external validation and acknowledgment is one of the most human things we do, especially when it comes to trauma.

When you've been hurt, silenced, or dismissed, it's natural to want someone to see your pain, to say, "I believe you," or "What happened to you matters."

Validation reassures us that our experiences are real and that we are not alone. But what happens when that validation doesn't come - when the people or systems we hoped would support us fall silent or refuse to acknowledge what we've endured? How do we move forward from trauma when the external world doesn't meet us where we need it to?

And why do so many of us seek validation from somewhere outside of ourselves?

At its core, the desire for validation stems from our need for connection. Humans are social beings, and much of our understanding of ourselves and our experiences comes from the way others respond to us. When you share your story or your pain, validation affirms that what you've been through is real, that it matters, and that you are worthy of care and support. It's a way of saying, "I see you, and you are not alone."

For those of you who have been through trauma, validation can feel especially crucial because trauma often leaves you questioning your reality.

I realised recently that I spent many years of my life seeking validation from others, despite the fact that I never got it. It really messed with me, and it took me a long time to realise that the validation I sought was never coming.

Like me, if your pain was dismissed or ignored at the time - by a perpetrator, a loved one, or even society - it can leave you doubting yourself:

'Did it really happen that way? Am I overreacting? Do I even deserve support? Does anyone even care what happened to me? Why was no one there for me?'

Getting the validation you need from others can help counteract those doubts, grounding you in the truth of your experience.

Acknowledgment also brings a sense of justice. When someone validates your trauma, it feels like a step toward accountability, a way of saying that what happened wasn't okay. This is why survivors often look to family, friends, or even institutions for acknowledgment - it feels like a way to begin the process of healing and repair.

Unfortunately, many people (like me) find that the validation and acknowledgment they long for doesn't come. People might downplay your experiences, avoid uncomfortable conversations, or outright deny what happened. Institutions might fail to hold perpetrators accountable or dismiss your story entirely. This lack of acknowledgment can feel like another layer of harm, compounding the pain of the original trauma.

It's important to remember that the absence of validation doesn't mean your experiences are invalid. Unfortunately, it is very common for some of us to never receive validation. It's a reflection of others' limitations, not of your truth.

People might struggle to validate your trauma because it forces them to confront their own discomfort, guilt, or complicity. Institutions often prioritise self-preservation over justice. These failures are about them, not you.

Moving forward without external validation can feel daunting, but it's entirely possible - and deeply empowering. It starts with the recognition that while validation from others can be comforting, it's not the only path to healing. You have the capacity to validate yourself, to honour your experiences, and to build a life that feels meaningful, even if others refuse to acknowledge your pain.

I had to do this myself, as I had no one and nowhere else to receive validation from. I have included some steps below to consider, but please do not feel as though this is something prescriptive.

1. Validate Yourself

Your experiences are valid because they happened, not because someone else says so. You don't need external permission to feel what you feel or to honour your pain. Self-validation means recognising your own truth, even in the absence of acknowledgment from others. It's saying to yourself, "I know what I went through. I know it mattered. And I know I deserve to heal."

This might feel difficult at first, especially if you've internalised doubt or blame. Start by gently reminding yourself that your feelings are valid, no matter what anyone else thinks. Journalling, positive affirmations, listening to music you relate to, or speaking to yourself with compassion can help reinforce this message.

2. Reconnect with Your Inner Voice

Trauma often silences our inner voice, making us doubt our instincts or question our reality. Our inner voice, our intuition and our instincts are all still there, but we sometimes ignore them, or we are taught to distrust them. Moving forward involves reconnecting with that voice and learning to trust it again.

Ask yourself:

What do I know to be true about my experiences?

What do I need to feel safe and supported?

Trusting your inner voice can be a powerful way to reclaim your sense of self.

3. Seek Support Where It Feels Safe

Even if validation doesn't come from the people or systems you hoped for, there are others who will see and honour your experiences. This might be a therapist, a support group, an online forum, or a trusted friend. It could also be connecting with stories from other survivors who've walked a similar path. Finding spaces where your pain is met with compassion can remind you that you are not alone.

4. Focus on What You Can Control

The lack of validation from others can feel like a loss of control, but healing involves shifting your focus to what's within your power. You can't control how others respond to your trauma, but you can control how you respond to yourself. This might mean prioritising self-care, setting boundaries, or exploring practices that help you feel grounded, like mindfulness or creative expression.

5. Redefine Healing

Healing doesn't require external validation - it requires self-compassion, courage, and the willingness to keep moving forward. It's about creating a life that feels fulfilling and authentic to you, regardless of whether others acknowledge your journey. Healing is a deeply personal process, and you get to define what it looks like.

While the lack of validation can feel like a heavy burden, it doesn't have to hold you back. Your life is not defined by the people or systems that failed to see you. It's defined by your resilience, your growth, and your ability to reclaim your story on your own terms.

Moving forward doesn't mean forgetting or pretending the pain didn't happen. It means recognising that your worth is not tied to others' acknowledgment. You are whole, you are enough, and you are capable of healing - even in the absence of external validation.

Remember, you are not alone in this journey.

There are people and communities who will stand beside you, who will see your strength and honour your truth. And most importantly, you have the power to honour yourself. Healing is possible, not because someone else grants it to you, but because you choose it for yourself.

Do you feel that you have had your traumatic experiences validated? Who validated those experiences?

Has there been anyone around you who has not validated your traumas? How did this impact your relationship with them?

Are there any traumas you have ignored, or not acknowledged for long periods of time, because they were too painful?

Have you ever had any justice for what happened to you? If yes, how did that impact you? If no, how has a lack of justice impacted you?

What do you feel you still need for closure around your trauma, and is it possible to get that closure?

How has it made you feel when your trauma has been minimised or trivialised by others?

Have you ever sought validation from someone else, only to feel judged? What happened?

If you still feel you have never truly been validated, what impact is that having on you now, and how are you coping?

Do you think there have been periods of your life when you have been struggling with unacknowledged traumas and distress that you were repressing? During that time, what were your thoughts and behaviours like?

If there was one person you could seek validation from, who would it be and why?

Do you think it would ever be possible to feel that 'justice was served' in relation to your own traumas? Why/why not?

Are there any traumas or experiences where you feel like you have not validated yourself? Where you haven't understood or explored it for yourself? If so, why do you feel you have never validated yourself?

Way to go! You completed the ninth step, 'Validating myself and my experiences'. Great work!

Write one thing you learned about yourself from this step.

Write one thing that challenged you to think differently in this step.

Use this space to tell yourself how far you have come since starting this programme. Celebrate your progress!

Step 10: Honouring the earlier version of myself

Welcome to the tenth step of *The Amethyst Programme!*

This step was so vital for me, and I wanted to share this with you all – as I feel it is such a transformative way of processing our trauma.

Honouring and respecting the younger versions of ourselves is a profoundly healing and loving act. I think this was one of the approaches that changed my life, especially as I carried so much shame about where I was from and how I grew up.

I can honestly say that I used to be embarrassed about who I was. I changed my name as soon as I could, when I was around 19 years old, because I desperately did not want to be known as Jessica Taylor anymore. When I used a different name, I felt free. I felt like I had moved on. Like I could shed my skin. Like I was able to disconnect myself from my trauma and my shame. I didn't have to be that teenage girl who was raped and got pregnant. I could be someone else. No one knew me. I even moved to a different part of the country (another very common experience for those of us who have been through trauma).

As you have probably noticed, I went back to my birth name in 2019, and whilst I was frightened about doing it, I truly felt like I was myself again. I wasn't ready to do it before then, but I am so glad I did. I love my name and my connection to my younger self now, but I didn't use to feel like this.

When we've been through trauma, it's easy to look back at the younger version of ourselves and feel pity, anger, or even shame. We might think, 'Why didn't I do something differently? Why didn't I see it coming? Why couldn't I handle it better?'

But the truth is, that younger version of you was doing the best they could with the knowledge, resources, and circumstances they had. Learning to love and honour them is not only an act of compassion - it's also a powerful way to process and understand your trauma and move forward with greater self-acceptance and peace.

It is vitally important that you do not project your current knowledge and wisdom on to an earlier version of yourself. There is absolutely nothing to gain from looking back and thinking, 'If I had known what I know now, I would never have done or said those things.'

You didn't know what you know now. You were not the same person. You have no way of going back there.

This energy is harmful to us all, and frankly, pointless. Instead, we could be doing the opposite – which is realising that we were younger, we were at a different stage in our evolution, we were in a different situation, with different people, and different circumstances. Instead of criticising ourselves and seeing that younger version as stupid or pathetic – we need to look back with compassion.

Trauma often leaves us with complicated feelings about our past. It's common to look back and feel regret, blame, or embarrassment for the choices we made or the things we endured. This is especially true if you were hurt in ways you didn't understand at the time, or if you responded to trauma in ways that you now feel ashamed of. Whether you defended and covered things up for your abuser, or a friend walked all over you for years – we can end up criticising and blaming that younger version of ourselves as if we were the problem!

But here's the thing: the younger you wasn't stupid, weak, naïve, or 'broken.' They were surviving. They were navigating a world that might not have felt safe, doing whatever they could to get through it.

Whether that meant trusting someone who betrayed you, staying quiet when you wanted to speak, or coping in ways that weren't always healthy, those responses weren't failures - they were survival strategies. Honouring your younger self means recognising the bravery it took to keep going, even when the odds were stacked against you.

Look at you now. You are here doing this programme for yourself, investing in your future, exploring your trauma, because of that younger version of yourself who pushed through unimaginable shit!

That younger version of you is the reason you are here today, ready to process and explore the trauma. Don't put them down, marvel at how on earth they managed to keep themselves going.

Trauma often leaves us feeling like our past is defined by pain or by what others did to us. By honouring your younger self, you can reclaim your narrative. Instead of seeing your past as a series of mistakes or things that 'happened to you,' you can choose to see it as a story of resilience and survival. That younger version of you endured things that no one should have to endure - and they made it through. That's worth honouring.

Are you proud of that younger version of yourself? Maybe you should be.

When you show compassion to your younger self, you're practising self-love in its purest form. You're saying, "You deserved better. I see your pain, and I'm here to support you now." This compassion can help soften feelings of shame or self-blame, replacing them with a sense of tenderness. It's a reminder that you didn't deserve what happened to you and that your worth has never been defined by your trauma.

The way you respond to the world today is often shaped by the experiences of your younger self. By honouring that version of you, you can better understand why certain things trigger you or why you've developed certain patterns.

For example, if your younger self learned that speaking up led to punishment, it makes sense that you might struggle with expressing your needs now. Recognising these connections allows you to approach your triggers with empathy rather than frustration.

Honouring your younger self also gives you the opportunity to reparent yourself. If the people around you didn't offer the love, protection, or guidance you needed, you can now step into that role for yourself. I know that can be hard, and a little exhausting. You can become the supportive, nurturing figure that your younger self longed for, offering them the care they deserved but may not have received.

Take time to reflect on what your younger self endured. What challenges did they face? What kept them going? How did they survive? What did they believe in? What distracted them? What made them happy? What made them stay in this world and keep going instead of giving up?

Instead of focusing on what you think they 'should' have done, focus on what they did to survive. Write them a letter, acknowledging their bravery and resilience, even if they didn't realise it at the time. This is something I did for myself, and even did it publicly at the end of my memoir, 'Underclass'.

Anyway, pay attention to how you talk about your past. Instead of saying, "I can't believe I let that happen," try, "I was doing the best I could with what I knew at the time." This shift in language can help you approach your past with more compassion.

Reconnecting with the things your younger self loved can be a beautiful way to honour them. Did they love drawing, dancing, or being in nature? Did they have favourite songs, books, or activities that brought them joy? Allow yourself to revisit those things, even if it feels silly or childlike. It's a way of saying, "Your happiness mattered then, and it matters now."

Honour your younger self by setting boundaries that protect their legacy. If they weren't able to stand up for themselves, you can do it now. If they endured relationships that hurt them, you can seek connections that feel safe and supportive today. Living in a way that honours their worth is a powerful act of healing.

When you think about painful moments from your past, imagine comforting your younger self as if you were there with them. This is a powerful approach, and something I have done several times. What would you say to your younger self? How would you hold or support them? What advice would you give them? How would they look at you? Would they listen? Were they ready? How could you show them love when they needed it most? Visualising this can create a sense of safety and closure, even for things that felt unbearable at the time.

Honouring your younger self isn't about dwelling on the past - it's about integrating it into your present in a way that feels kind and empowering. It's about recognising that every version of you, no matter how scared or hurt, was worthy of love and care. And it's about carrying that love forward, creating a life that honours their resilience and dreams.

When you love your younger self, you create a bridge between who you were and who you are becoming. You remind yourself that you've always been worthy, that your pain doesn't define you, and that healing is possible. It's not about erasing the struggles - they're part of your story - but about holding them with compassion and using them as a foundation for growth.

Your younger self deserves to be honoured, not judged. And the more you offer them love and understanding, the more you'll find yourself moving toward a future that feels grounded in self-compassion, strength, and hope.

You are both the survivor of your past and the creator of your future - and that's a truly powerful thing.

List some common ways that people disrespect earlier
versions of themselves when going through trauma. Do you
think you have ever done this yourself?

Write about a part of your trauma that you still feel embarrassed or ashamed of, when you know you shouldn't.

If the present day You could see a past version of You in trauma, what would you see? How would you help her?

Sometimes we apply knowledge and wisdom we have now to younger versions of ourselves and then get upset or angry that we didn't understand or 'see the signs' of a situation. Do you relate to this at all?

What do you think the impact is on us disrespecting that
earlier version of ourselves going through trauma?

What would you have to change in order for you to love and
honour that earlier version of yourself?

Is there anything you feel you need to forgive yourself for?
Write about this here.

Write about how amazing that earlier version of yourself was.
What do you need to thank her for?

If you met that earlier version of yourself and could speak to her for just a few minutes, what would you say to her?

Is there anything you need to stop blaming and shaming yourself for? Write about this here.

When it comes to trauma, do you see or describe yourself as a victim, a survivor, none, or both? How do you feel about this kind of language?

Way to go! You completed the tenth step, 'Honouring the earlier version of myself'. How are you feeling?

Write one thing you learned about yourself from this step.

Write one thing that challenged you to think differently in this step.

Use this space to encourage yourself to work through this programme. Tell yourself how well you are doing!

Step 11: Reconnecting with myself – who am I now?

Hey! It's Jaimi here.

Having been through my own personal experiences of reconnecting with myself and exploring who I am during and after trauma, we thought I could drop by and write to you all on this one.

You're here at step eleven of *The Amethyst Programme*, and in this step, we are going to explore what it feels like to reconnect to ourselves after feeling so detached for so long.

Who are we after everything we went through? Will we ever be the same again? Do we even want to be?

This step is all about learning about yourself and reconnecting at a deeper level. You've changed – and that's okay.

During trauma, and during the aftermath as we navigate our own processing of trauma and distress, many of us have to disconnect from parts of ourselves and our lives while we focus on surviving.

When I look back on periods of trauma and trauma processing in my life, I can retrospectively see that my life felt clouded and dazed. So much energy was taken up on my emotions, and so much time was spent navigating what I would previously have considered basic tasks.

So, when we come to reconnect with ourselves after trauma, and as life starts to feel more 'normal' again, some of this may feel like getting to know ourselves again, and some of this will be getting to know a new version of ourselves.

Learning who we are

Learning about ourselves is the process of becoming aware of our thoughts, feelings, behaviours, and motivations. It involves reflection, introspection, and the ability to recognise patterns, events, relationships, and wider experiences in our lives that shape our identity and decisions.

When we learn about ourselves, it can help us to gain clarity on our values, strengths, and areas for growth, which can lead to a greater sense of self-understanding, which is often strived for in attempts to gain self-control and liberation, as well as connecting with our true authentic selves.

As human beings, we are shaped and moulded by our environment and experiences which change frequently, leading to alterations in our perspective, which in turn, may change core parts of ourselves such as our character and behaviour.

People often talk about 'finding themselves' as if this is a singular discovery or destination, but what is more likely, is that we 'find ourselves' over and over again throughout our lives, as we ourselves change, shift, and mould - especially those of us who prioritise, or are on a journey to self-awareness.

Poet Mahmoud Darwish once said, "You will never find the same person twice. Not even in the same person."

I love that quote.

Every individual you meet, including ourselves, are evolving; on one end of the spectrum, that may be becoming more static and concrete in thinking, perspectives, and behaviour all becoming more embedded, or the other end, reimagining, re-looking at, and altering all aspects of our character, behaviour, thoughts and beliefs.

There is of course what is most common, somewhere in the middle of this metaphorical spectrum. Most of us will sit here the majority of our lives, with parts of ourselves that stay very similar (such as general cultural outlooks, perhaps a favourite colour, music genre, or dish) and parts of ourselves that are most likely to change (conflict style, how we view relationships, your favourite memory).

Of course, these will be very different from person to person.

Experiencing trauma can significantly alter our sense of self and the way we interact with, and perceive the world around us- core parts of who we are. It's likely that different types of traumas will change an individual in different ways.

For example, you are more likely to see sudden and big character, behaviour, and belief changes in somebody who has recently experienced or been subjected to acute trauma (such as a car crash, rape, or near-death experience), or indeed a sudden realisation of trauma (such as realising you were abused as a child).

However, when people are subjected to or experience chronic trauma (such as long-term health issues, oppression, abuse, or career-related vicarious trauma such as being in the emergency services) you are more likely to see slower changes in the person's character, behaviour, and beliefs due to the cumulative, but frequent level of trauma the individual is dealing with. They may become less compassionate, their humour may change, relate to others in a different way to how they did previously.

Post-Traumatic Growth

Something that traumatises us holds significance in our lives to us as individuals. When something holds significance in our lives, especially when that is an event, or series of events, it is unlikely to be 'normal' or 'your normal'- otherwise it would likely be insignificant in comparison to any other part of your life.

Trauma often compels us to reevaluate our identity and ways of functioning, sometimes resulting in profound personal growth or shifts in perspective. While it is essential to hold those who harmed us fully accountable, validate the harm we experienced, and acknowledge its impact, the concept of post-traumatic growth can still hold immense value for our healing journey.

Post-traumatic growth refers to the advancements we make after trauma, often brought on by the way trauma has changed us. For example, many people who have had a near-death experience will report having a new-found desire to make the most out of life, which often includes spending more time with loved ones, doing nice things for themselves, shifting their lifestyles to one that takes better care of their body.

For some people, post-traumatic growth can feel like new-found inner strength, new beginnings, and putting yourself first…and so as I am at risk of quoting the entirety of Kelly Clarkson's 'What Doesn't Kill You', I'll leave the examples there.

As you move through this section, you'll be given the chance to reflect on post-traumatic growth.

Perhaps think about examples of how you've seen this portrayed in art, music, and media. Are there parts that you relate to? And parts you don't? The reason I ask, is when considering the concept of post-traumatic growth, we must be aware of toxic positivity. The two can appear and sound very similar. Toxic positivity promotes an unconditional positive mindset which often invalidates and silences parts of ourselves that are hurting or have been harmed. It can cause stigmatisation and taboo around valid feelings of upset, injustice, pain, helplessness, and struggle which can lead to further psychological harm. To avoid spilling into toxic positivity, ensure you validate your own feelings and acknowledge their presence, don't minimise them, and don't feel as though you must 'stay positive' and 'look on the bright side' all of the time.

What remained from our character and personality pre-trauma

It's likely that lots of parts of you will stay the same before and after experiencing and processing trauma. It can be really useful to reflect and consider what these are for you, to help you identify core parts of yourself.

While core parts of ourselves can change throughout our lives, and indeed following trauma, what remains of ourselves after distress, trauma, or a huge shakeup in our life, is a good indication of who we are at present. Those parts of us got us through that period of trauma, and indeed the longer-term aftermath we may still be navigating.

What we lose from trauma

Trauma takes so much away from us. It can strip us of our sense of safety, trust in others, and belief in the world as a fair and predictable place. It might rob us of certain relationships, as some people may not understand or know how to support us through our pain. Some of those people may even have directly caused us pain and trauma.

We can lose confidence in ourselves, our abilities, or the goals we once dreamt of achieving. Often, trauma alters how we see ourselves - leaving us feeling broken, disconnected, or distant from who we once were. This loss can feel overwhelming, like a part of us has been permanently taken away. However, it's important to remember that while trauma takes much, it doesn't define all of who we are. Over time, with processing and reflection, we can begin to reclaim parts of ourselves, and rebuild a life that honours both our past and our resilience.

What we gain from trauma

When humans are in traumatic situations or periods of our lives, we can often surprise ourselves with the skills we develop or the skills that are enhanced during this, to cope and/or survive. These skills can stay with us for life and can help us navigate our own trauma processing, and other situations in the future.

For example, becoming more vigilant and aware of our surroundings and potential dangers can help you keep safe in unrelated situations and avoid harm. Maybe you're able to stay calm and think more strategically in high-pressure situations - meaning you've developed a heightened ability to respond to a crisis. In addition to this, coping mechanisms such as hobbies or creative expressions can often develop during trauma. Maybe you started writing short poems in the notes section of your phone, or an ability to analyse lyrics written by hundreds of musicians when you sought out connection. Maybe you began learning an instrument or a new sport. Maybe the trauma left you with a sense of duty and a desire to pursue advocacy and activism.

How to reconnect with the new version of ourselves after trauma, even when we want to go back to who we used to be

Reconnecting with ourselves after trauma can feel like navigating unfamiliar territory, especially when we long to return to the person we were before. You'll never be the person you were before the trauma, and that's because humans are supposed to change with experiences. It's what keeps us safe, and what makes us who we are as individuals. It's important to recognise that while we can't undo what has happened, we have the power to shape who we are now and who we want to become.

It's important that we don't put pressure on ourselves to 'go back to normal' or be the same person we once were.

Reconnecting with ourselves, in the same way we would an old friend is about listening (to yourself) and learning to embrace the person you've become while nurturing the parts of yourself that have remained. This process allows you to rebuild and grow into a version of yourself that honours both the pain you've endured and the resilience you've built.

What have you learned about yourself whilst working through
The Amethyst Programme so far?

How would you describe yourself when you were going through trauma versus how you would describe yourself today?

Which parts of yourself have remained consistent and similar throughout all the traumatic experiences you have had?

Which parts of yourself do you feel you have lost through
trauma?

Which parts of yourself do you feel you gained from, or through, trauma?

Are there any parts of yourself that you recognise you lost through trauma, but you don't want back? Why is that?

Are there any parts of yourself that you now have from trauma, that you wish you didn't have? Why is that?

Write five things you love about yourself below. Don't roll your eyes at me! Who are you? What do you love about yourself?

What do you need to thank yourself for? Write a letter to yourself here.

What do you need to thank your body for? Write a letter to your body here.

What do you enjoy doing, and what makes you happy these days? Write a list here.

What was your proudest moment? Why are you proud of that
moment in particular?

**Write a list of your skills and talents. I know you have them!
What are you good at?**

When was the last time you did something just for you? Something that brought you joy and peace. Write about it here. Do more of that!

Write five reasons why you want to reconnect with your inner self after trauma.

Awesome work! You completed the eleventh step,
'Reconnecting with myself'. Brilliant progress!

Write one thing you learned about yourself from this step.

Write one thing that challenged you to think differently in this step.

Use this space to encourage yourself to work through this programme. Tell yourself how fantastic you are doing!

Step 12: Changing my habits and patterns after trauma

Oof! It's a big step, this one. But I have faith in you!

Welcome to your twelfth step of thirteen, and the one where we explore our habits, our patterns and our negative self-talk. We've all got to do it! And as I always say, 'If nothing changes, nothing changes!'

Let's work together, and talk it through.

I hope to cover the following topics in this step, and there are lots of reflective exercises for you to explore further. We will discuss self-talk, catastrophic thoughts, hearing voices, and bullying ourselves. We will talk about how those habits and coping mechanisms embed, and how to explore them in more detail – in a way that doesn't pathologise or judge us.

Ready? Okay.

You are not lost, you are evolving. Evolution requires change, and change is ultimately why you are here. If we stay stuck in our traumas, we feel terrible, we lose years of our lives, and we never truly honour ourselves and what we deserve after trauma.

One of the most common things that people say to me about their lives after trauma, is that they feel totally lost. They reach a point where they don't know what they want anymore. They don't recognise themselves. They don't know which way they want to go. They hate their jobs. They question their marriage. They wonder who their real friends are. They dream of a different kind of life. They want peace. They want love. They want joy. They want to expand, grow and explore. They want to understand themselves and they want to know how to move forwards.

The first thing I always say is that whilst this feeling might be overwhelming, there are two ways of looking at it:

1. You are lost, you have no map, you have no idea what you are doing, and you are frightened that you can't cope.

OR

2. You are at a crossroads in your life because you are going through a period of growth due to trauma. This is your evolution. This is your time to make some choices about the next direction in your life. This is the time to make changes.

Look at those again. They are very different ways of looking at a period of crisis in our lives, aren't they?

One keeps us stuck and hopeless, and the other one gives us the freedom to respect and love ourselves through a period of our lives where we might need to stop, reevaluate, and decide how to move forward.

One thing I have learned in my own life is that our words will change our lives. The stories we tell ourselves, about ourselves, and about what happened to us, change the way we see everything. If we tell ourselves that we are useless, that we are lost, that we will never get over this, and we cannot see a future where we are happy, we are unlikely to ever change anything. We are putting ourselves down. We are talking to ourselves like we mean nothing. And so many of us do this every single day.

But what happens when we start talking to ourselves in terms of growth, evolution, change, moving forward, trusting and loving ourselves? I know for me, this changed my life many years ago. I also know that when I slip back into negative thinking and self-talk patterns, I grind to a halt.

All about self-talk

I'm so stupid. I'm fat. I'm ugly. I will never get over this. I shouldn't have let this happen to me. I should have seen it coming. I'm such an idiot. Why do I let people walk all over me? I hate my body. I am so useless. I never get anything right. No one likes me anyway. I should just quit, I'm not good at anything. I have nothing to offer anyone. I'm worthless. I'm boring. I'm such a loser. I have done nothing with my life. No one would want someone like me anyway. I'm not strong enough. I'm not smart enough. I'm not sexy enough. I'm not a good daughter. I don't deserve love. I will end up alone.

Sound familiar?

Experiencing trauma can leave us feeling vulnerable, shaken, and often overwhelmed by our inner dialogue. Negative self-talk is a common response after a traumatic event. While these thoughts can feel automatic and convincing, it's important to understand their roots and impact.

Negative self-talk often stems from our mind's way of trying to make sense of what happened. After a traumatic event, our minds may replay the situation repeatedly, searching for control or understanding. This can lead to self-blame or harsh judgments about how we acted - or didn't act - in the moment. While this process is a natural part of coping, unchecked negative self-talk can keep us stuck in a cycle of guilt, shame, and low self-esteem.

The impact of these thoughts on our well-being can be significant.

I mean, just look back at them! They are horrific to see in black and white. And I bet some of us have said much, much worse to ourselves.

I would go as far as saying that we have probably said worse things to ourselves than we ever have to someone else.

This level of negative self-talk will increase feelings of trauma and worthlessness, interfere with our ability to trust ourselves or others, and even make it harder to move forward. Over time, self-talk like this can affect how we see ourselves and the world, reinforcing a belief that we are somehow unworthy or broken.

The good news is that with awareness and support, we can challenge and change these patterns.

Start by noticing when these thoughts arise and gently questioning them. Ask yourself, "Would I speak to a loved one this way?" Often, we are far kinder to others than we are to ourselves.

Remember, the negative self-talk isn't your truth - it's a reflection of your pain. With compassion and patience, you can begin to rewrite that narrative and reclaim your strength.

So much of what we say to ourselves is bullying and abusive. I realised this myself several years back, and felt sadness. The things I have said to myself, the things I have thought — what impact have I had, when I could be the one person telling myself positive, loving, encouraging and reassuring messages?

Once I stopped myself, and challenged my own patterns, I noticed how much better I felt when I used positive affirmations and messages to myself. I shudder to think how low I kept myself by talking so badly about, and to, myself for so long.

Catastrophic thoughts

Trauma can profoundly impact how we process the world, often amplifying our fears and creating catastrophic thoughts. These thoughts can feel sudden, vivid, and alarming - like worrying we might throw ourselves in front of a train or crash our car, even when we know deep down that we don't want to. This disconnect between what we feel and what we actually desire can be deeply unsettling.

I have had these thoughts myself many times, and I have met thousands of people who have these thoughts too. Some people have the most outrageous catastrophic thoughts, such as imagining themselves drop kicking a baby across a park, and some people have dark catastrophic thoughts about killing their own family members. In each example, the person is horrified by their own thoughts, and cannot understand why they happen.

Such catastrophic thoughts are often rooted in the brain's natural response to trauma. After a traumatic event, our brain's survival mechanisms become hyperactive, constantly scanning for danger.

Not only do we scan for danger, but we create dangerous examples in our mind, to almost say to ourselves, 'What if this happened? What would you do?'

This heightened state can lead to intrusive thoughts that feel extreme or out of character. They aren't a reflection of your true intentions - they're your brain's way of rehearsing worst-case scenarios to try to keep you safe. It's as if your mind is over-preparing for situations it perceives as risky, even when the actual risk is low. Or non-existent.

The impact of these thoughts can be distressing, though. They may leave you feeling scared, embarrassed, ashamed, isolated, or even questioning your sense of control. You might avoid situations like driving or traveling on trains, fearing the thoughts themselves, rather than any real desire to act on them. Over time, this avoidance can shrink your world and make it harder to reclaim your confidence.

It's crucial to remember that these thoughts, while distressing, are a normal response to trauma - not a sign that something is wrong with you. Gently acknowledging these thoughts without judgment can help reduce their power. Techniques like grounding exercises, naming the thought as "just a thought," or working with a trauma-informed therapist or programme can be incredibly supportive.

Most importantly, remind yourself: catastrophic thoughts do not define your intentions, character, or future. They are a symbol of what you've been through, not who you are. With time and support, they can lose their grip, and you can regain trust in yourself

Hearing voices and your intuition

When we've been through trauma, it's not uncommon to notice a heightened awareness of inner voices - our own voice, someone else's voice, our intuition, or even messages that feel like they're coming from somewhere deeper within. Far from being dangerous or abnormal, this can be a powerful and meaningful aspect of how our mind and body process trauma and begin to heal.

Trauma often disrupts our sense of connection with ourselves. In response, the mind can develop new ways of communicating what needs attention. Inner voices might emerge as a way of expressing emotions, unmet needs, or insights that haven't yet found another outlet. These voices can take different forms: a gentle reminder to rest, a protective warning in uncertain situations, or even a reflection of unspoken fears or hopes.

Far from being 'wrong', 'psychotic' or pathological, these voices often carry wisdom. They might speak to parts of ourselves that we've disconnected from - a younger self longing for safety, or our intuitive self, guiding us toward healing. By listening without judgment, we can begin to understand what these messages are trying to tell us.

The experience of hearing inner voices can feel unsettling at first, especially if trauma has made it hard to trust ourselves. But these voices are not here to harm you; they're part of your natural capacity to make sense of what you've been through. Practicing grounding techniques, journaling about what you hear, or exploring these experiences with a trauma-informed mentor or guide can help you build trust in your inner world.

Remember, your intuition and inner voice are powerful allies. They are signs of your resilience and your body's natural wisdom, guiding you back to connection, safety, and wholeness. With time, these messages can become a source of clarity, strength, and healing.

Do you feel ready to make changes to the way you think and talk about yourself?

What do you think the impact has been from talking and thinking in negative ways about yourself?

Write out your most common negative self-talk phrases and thoughts. Fill this page with them. Take a look at them, and describe the impact this is having on you.

When did you start putting yourself down, or having negative thoughts about yourself? Why do you think you started doing that?

Do you have intrusive thoughts or catastrophic thoughts? List the most repetitive ones here.

Look back at your list of intrusive and catastrophic thoughts
– what do you think they really mean? What are they telling
you about what you are really feeling?

Do you hear voices in your mind? Write about what they say here, and describe them. Are they your voice, or someone else's? What do they say? When do they happen, and when do they lessen? Do you see any patterns or connections in your answers?

When I start thinking negative or harmful things about myself, what can I do differently to redirect my thoughts, distract myself with something positive, correct my thoughts, or challenge myself?

If you doubt yourself and your ideas or ambitions, when did this start? Why do you think you do this?

Are there any thoughts or talk about yourself that you now recognise need to change? List them here.

Are there situations, people or other triggers who seem to increase your intrusive or catastrophic thoughts? Why do you think this is?

Have you ever been frightened of your own thoughts, voices and beliefs? How has this fear stopped you from processing the related traumas?

What myths do you feel you have believed about hearing voices, or negative, intrusive or catastrophic thoughts? How have these myths impacted you?

How many of your negative thoughts and voices arise from people who have abused you and put you down? Have you internalised messages and voices of others?

Which of your coping mechanisms need to change, and why?

Way to go! You completed the twelfth step, 'Changing my habits and patterns after trauma'. How are you feeling?

Write one thing you learned about yourself from this step.

Write one thing that challenged you to think differently in this step.

Use this space to encourage yourself to work through this programme. Tell yourself how well you are doing!

Step 13: Loving myself through lifelong processing

Welcome to the final step of The Amethyst Programme!

I hope you are feeling super proud of yourself today. You worked through so much, and now you are here at the thirteenth step – which is all about loving yourself through trauma as it weaves through our lives, as we age and grow and evolve.

I know with so many programmes and therapies, the goal is to get you to a place where the trauma has ended, or you are no longer affected by the traumatic experiences – but I just don't think that is very realistic.

We carry our memories and experiences with us for the rest of our lives. There is no 'end', in that sense.

Trauma recovery is not linear, but it is not a life sentence

We have been duped when it comes to the way trauma is talked about. Many of us find that we come to a point in our lives where we have our head in our hands, and we ask, "Why haven't I got over this yet? Why does this keep coming back to haunt me? Why do I feel like I am going backwards?"

I truly believe that these questions come from misconceptions about trauma processing and healing. We are generally fed a smooth, shiny programme of 'treatment' in which we acknowledge we have a problem, we go to therapy, we break it all down, talk about our problems, and then the suffering goes away – and we go back to being our normal happy selves. Or in the case of psychiatry, we go to the doctor, they give us some pills, we take them every day, our feelings go away, and we feel right as rain again. Problem solved.

So, when the same feelings, fears and memories pop back up ten years later, or when your kids are born, or when your mum dies, or when your marriage breaks down – you can find yourself questioning whether you were ever truly 'healed'.

So, as you end this programme, I want to reassure you about something: it is common, normal, and totally understandable that your trauma memories and feelings will come back up to be reprocessed several times in your life.

You are not broken. You are not relapsing. You are not disordered.

Our journey through and from trauma is not a straight line from A to B. Trauma becomes part of the rich tapestry of who we are, and if we are led to believe that we can just cut that bit out and forget about it, we will never move forward healthily. Try not to be frightened by this idea, as I hope to show you that not only is this completely normal, but it is an important part of your life.

Was it a nice part of your life? Fuck no. Can you erase it? Also no.

Has it become a part of you and your life journey? Well, yes. It already has.

Triggering parts of life

Life has a weird way of saying to you, 'Hey! Remember that thing you thought you had processed and resolved? Well, lets think about it all over again, but this time, here is a new memory you forgot about!'

Or my personal favourite (not)…

'Hey! Remember this thing that happened to you, well here's some information you didn't have the first time around, and now you need to completely reprocess the entire experience all over again, but from a different angle!'

I want to reassure you that when this comes up for you, (and it will), you are going to be fine. You might need to take some time for yourself, honour yourself again, remind yourself of everything in this programme, and you might need some support – but you are going to get through it.

Our memories are processed and reprocessed. This is normal. Our memories are not static files that are stored, like photos and videos in our phone. They change and reshape based on our knowledge and perceptions – so as we change, we are likely to reprocess our memories, and understand them differently.

For example, you may believe you had a pretty normal upbringing until you watch a documentary on TV about childhood abuse and neglect, realise that you were abused as a child, and then see your parents through a completely different lens.

You might have children, and suddenly realise that your mother was manipulative and cold. You might meet a new partner and realise your ex was sexually abusive towards you. You might get a new job and realise you were terrified of your last boss.

Life will continue these journeys for you, and you will continue to grow and evolve, if you allow it to happen.

Simply put, there are going to be many parts of your life that trigger your stuff again, and maybe even cause you to reevaluate what you thought you knew – but it you stay anchored to your inner self, and your trust in your resilience, you will be able to work through it and process it just like you did before. Just like you are doing now.

You are not going backwards, you are not 'relapsing'.

Every step is forwards, I promise.

Traumas that remain unresolved

It is important to talk about the traumas that are super hard to process or resolve. I don't want to finish writing this programme without acknowledging the fact that for some of us, there will be traumas that remain unresolved for us for long periods of our lives.

If you have traumas that still feel too raw, it might not be the right time to work through them. Also, if you are in a dangerous or unstable environment at the moment that is very stressful or demanding, you may find that now is not the right moment to unearth unresolved stuff that might be too heavy.

Alternatively, it might be that the trauma is unresolved because you have no closure, or you need further information and validation in order to move on.

Whilst this is all totally valid and natural, I do want to speak frankly, if I may.

Sometimes, our unresolved traumas will show up in ways that we don't fully understand yet. We might get super triggered by a certain behaviour in our partner, and not even know why. We might blow up over something, and feel entitled to do so, but then regret it.

We might think we have behaved reasonably, when everyone else is telling us that we mishandled something, or treated someone terribly.

We might believe we are worthless or shit at something, when everyone else is telling us that we are brilliant and talented.

We might look in the mirror and see ugliness. We might hate our bodies and our face. We might tell ourselves that we are too fat and too old – whilst everyone around us struggles to see what we can see.

Experiences like this are usually signs of something unprocessed or unresolved. As an example of what I mean, and to be completely transparent, I still have unresolved trauma around my appearance and my body due to years of being abused and told I am ugly and fat by family, exes, abusers and strangers.

One of the ways this seems to show up for me, is that I cannot stand to be in conversations with women talking about how much they hate their body and how much they want to lose weight. I either disassociate, or end up snapping at someone. I hadn't actually noticed this behaviour until my wife pointed it out to me, and it has taken me five years to recover some unprocessed memories that explain where that comes from. Five bloody years.

Our unresolved stuff can sit just under the surface, and influence and guide our behaviour, our triggers, our reactions and our thoughts without us even knowing – so bare that in mind too, as you continue on your journey after this programme.

Do you have a particular trauma or memory that seems to pop back up every now and then? Why do you think that might be happening?

Are there any traumas you feel you will never 'get over'? Are you comfortable with that?

Describe how you can demonstrate more patience with yourself when you are getting triggered.

How do you feel about the messy and non-linear nature of trauma processing in a world where everything is expected to be linear and neat?

As we are coming to the end of The Amethyst Programme, can you list the traumas that you feel are still unresolved for you?

If you do have unresolved traumas, what can you do to work on your feelings and memories of them?

How does it make you feel when you hear someone say, 'Trauma does not define you, but it is part of you'?

Are there specific dates or events that trigger you back to a certain trauma? How will you care for yourself when those dates or events come around?

How do you feel about the fact that our trauma memories are memories just like any other, and we are likely to be triggered back to them in lots of ways throughout life?

How do you feel about me saying that the trauma was an important part of your life?

Can you list some milestones in your own life that seemed to trigger your trauma responses and coping mechanisms that you thought were resolved?

How do you think constantly trying to avoid thinking about
the traumatic times in our lives impacts us?

How do you feel about the idea that trauma gets processed and reprocessed over and over again as our thinking evolves over the lifespan? Do you resonate with this at all?

Way to go! You completed the thirteenth and final step, 'Loving myself through lifelong processing'.

You did it! You completed The Amethyst Programme!

Write one thing you learned about yourself from this step.

Write one thing that challenged you to think differently in this step.

Use this space to encourage yourself to work through this programme. Tell yourself how well you are doing!

Final thoughts

Ah! I am so proud of you for getting through the programme in your own time, in your own way. This is exactly how I wanted it to be, and I hope you have learned tonnes about yourself along the way. Be proud of yourself. Most people never reflect to this depth!

You have chosen to invest time, love, and thought into your life and into your future by completing this programme – and these are some of the most powerful gifts you could ever give yourself after trauma.

I hope this programme has also demonstrated that trauma can be processed and explored on our own terms, in our own words, and in our own ways. The power of knowledge cannot be understated.

We are not taught to explore ourselves in this depth, and I often think there is a reason for that. Many people don't feel like they truly know themselves, but then again, they have never invested any time in reflecting on their lives, their behaviours, thoughts and feelings.

You've done something brilliant for yourself here, and I hope you can come back to this programme whenever you need it.

All the best for your future!

Dr Jessica Taylor

xxx

Learn more about what I do at

www.drjessicataylor.com and www.victimfocus.com

Catch me on social media, under @DrJessTaylor on pretty much everything.

Final reflections

Use this space to reflect on how you are feeling since completing The Amethyst Programme.

What have you learned about yourself?

List three things you now think differently about

your trauma and your experiences

Reflect on how you feel about your trauma

responses and coping mechanisms

after completing the programme

List five things you want to change since

completing this programme

By the same author

Taylor, J. (2024) The Watcher of Your Own Flame: Understanding and nurturing yourself after trauma

Taylor, J. (2024) Underclass: A Memoir, Hachette, Little, Brown Publications, London

Taylor, J. & Shrive, J. (2023) The Indicative Trauma Impact Manual, VictimFocus Publications, London

Taylor, J. (2022) Sexy but Psycho: How patriarchy uses women's trauma against them, Hachette, Little, Brown Publications, London

Taylor, J. (2020) Why Women are Blamed for Everything: Exposing the culture of victim blaming, Hachette, Little, Brown Publications, London

Taylor, J. (2020) The Reflective Journal For Parents and Carers: Supporting your child after sexual abuse, VictimFocus

Taylor, J. & Shrive, J. (2020) The Primary School & Home School Guide: Ethical sex and relationships education for young children, VictimFocus

Taylor, J. (2020) Woman in Progress: The Reflective Journal for Women and Girls Subjected to Abuse and Trauma, VictimFocus

Taylor, J. (2020) The Reflective Journal for Researchers and Academics, VictimFocus

Taylor, J. (2019) The Reflective Journal for Practitioners Working in Trauma and Abuse, VictimFocus

Printed in Great Britain
by Amazon

56335693R00182